FORAGE IN AUTUMN

THE FOOD AND MEDICINE OF BRITAIN'S WILD PLANTS

ROBIN HARFORD

Copyright © 2023 by Robin Harford

Robin Harford has asserted his rights as author of this work in accordance with the Copyright, Designs and Patents Act 1988.

All rights reserved. No part of this publication may be reproduced, stored in a retrieval system, or transmitted, in any form, by any means, electronic, mechanical, photocopying, recording or otherwise, without written permission of the publisher unless in accordance with the provisions of the Copyright Designs and Patents Act 1988.

Great care has been taken to maintain the accuracy of the information contained in this work. However, neither the publisher, the editor nor author can be held responsible for any consequences arising from use of the information contained herein. The views expressed in this work are those of the author and do not necessarily reflect those of the publisher.

ISBN: 978-1-915823-05-2

Second edition

Eatweeds Press, Exeter, Devon, UK

For the green ones

CONTENTS

Introduction — vii
Safety and sustainability guidelines — ix

1. Beech — 1
2. Blackthorn (Sloe) — 14
3. Crab Apple — 25
4. Dog Rose (Rosehip) — 38
5. Guelder Rose — 57
6. Hawthorn — 68
7. Hazel — 84
8. Horseradish — 96
9. Oak — 113
10. Rowan — 134
11. Sea Buckthorn — 146
12. Strawberry Tree — 159
13. Sweet Chestnut — 171
14. Wild Service Tree — 188
15. Wood Avens — 201

About the Author — 211
Bibliography — 213

INTRODUCTION

It is my intention to help you become a plant ambassador. Someone who loves their local flora enough to want to protect it and be a voice for the plants.

My plant mentor Frank Cook always said:

> If you know one plant really well, then teach it to others.

This is how we spread our love of plants. It isn't about becoming an expert or a teacher per se, it is about changing the culture, one plant at a time.

Our plant heritage is slowly being forgotten and it is people like you who can change that.

Start sharing what you learn within the pages of this book with others.

Create wild food meals and ask your friends and loved ones over. Take them out plant spotting. Bring the wildness of the world into your home. Surround yourself with green.

See this as a journey down the Green Path. An exciting adventure. Become a playful plant explorer. Enjoy the ride. It's going to be a blast.

I hope some day our paths will cross, until then, happy gathering.

SAFETY AND SUSTAINABILITY GUIDELINES

Foraging is all about sustainability.

The relationship between plants and people.

How we engage with the natural world without violating it.

Humans are grazing animals and have as much right to be in the ecosystem as any other animal.

The hysterical newspaper headlines and armchair conservationists shout that foragers are evil pillagers who destroy habitats and biodiversity.

> According to the UK State of Nature report, issued in September 2019 by a grouping of over seventy nature conservation organisations, the major pressures on the UK's nature are: unsustainable forms of agricultural and woodland management, climate change, urbanisation, pollution, hydrological change and invasive non-native species.
>
> — BIODIVERSITY IN THE UK: BLOOM OR BUST? A HOUSE OF COMMONS COMMITTEE REPORT

Foragers are some of the most ecologically aware people around and are deeply embedded with their environment.

You don't destroy what you love, care and have respect for.

SUSTAINABLE HARVESTING GUIDELINES

Here is my advice so you can become a responsible, safe and sustainable forager.

- Try and harvest away from other humans. Some people think picking any wildflower is illegal. It isn't. This minimises the possibility for potential confrontation. See https://www.eatweeds.co.uk/foraging-and-the-law

- Only gather what you will use today and maybe tomorrow. One in ten (10%) is the best ratio to go by. This leaves most of the plant stand (community) for other non-humans and has a minimal impact on the ecosystem.

If you go over this you are gathering from plant communities that are too small.

Every plant is different in how much harvesting it can tolerate. Some thrive when harvested heavily. Others will be impacted and might decline.

Foraging requires paying close attention to how your harvesting protocols impact your local land-base. Each plant and ecosystem is unique.

- Only harvest perennials. Picking them does not usually threaten their survival.

- Never harvest endangered, rare or threatened species.

A plant might be recorded as scarce or rare in one county yet grow in abundance in another. Know the local status of a plant.

- Contact a local botany group and go through your list of plants with someone there. See https://bsbi.org/local-botany

- Learn the flora in your county. Approach this as a journey, an exciting game. Become a plant explorer. See https://bsbi.org/county-floras

THE GOLDEN RULES

- Never eat any plant you do not have a 100% positive identification for. This means you are absolutely certain you have the correct plant.

- If you catch yourself thinking - "I think it is" - you do not know.

- If in doubt, leave it out. Never munch on a hunch.

LEARN TO FORAGE SAFELY

If you'd like to deepen your foraging skills, why not come on one of my foraging courses. Details can be found at:

https://www.eatweeds.co.uk/foraging-courses

WHAT THE PRESS ARE SAYING

'Highly rated' - The Guardian

'A revelation!' - BBC Good Food Magazine

'One of Britain's most dedicated foragers' - The Lady

BEECH
Fagus sylvatica

FAMILY

Fagaceae

BOTANICAL DESCRIPTION

Height: 3 to 45 metres. Flowers: male flowers are numerous and tassel-like, female flowers are arranged in pairs in erect clusters. Bark: smooth, grey bark. Leaves: oval leaves of bright, translucent green with 5–9 pairs of veins, wavy margins fringed with hairs and fine hairs underneath leaves. Fruit: fruit cupule contains 1–2 shiny, brown nuts.

FLOWERS

April to May.

STATUS

Perennial. Native.

HABITAT

Woodland on calcareous soils, in forests, parks, avenues, and hedges.

OVERVIEW

The Beech belongs to the same family as the Oak and chestnut – Fagaceae. Its species name of *Fagus sylvatica* refers to the tree's woodland habitat.

There are differences of opinion about its arrival in Britain. Some sources lean heavily on the report of the Gallic wars in De Bello Gallico by Julius Caesar (100–44 BC), who said there were no Beech trees in Britain and that the Beech must have been introduced during the Roman occupation.

Other sources suggest that Caesar did not see enough of the British Isles to know any better. Archaeological finds of Beech pollen in peat deposits suggest that Beech trees arrived in Britain long before the Romans did.

The story of Beech includes more than 100 uses for its wood, bark, leaves, flowers and nuts. If you can't find a use for Beech in your home and garden, then enjoy its decorative features in parks and remember to appreciate its shade in summer.

Be warned. The Beech is easily displeased, so mind your language and don't swear lest the tree drops a branch.

FOOD

An ancient Greek belief is that Beechnuts, called 'mast', were the first food eaten by humans and thus, the name Fagus is derived from the Greek phago, meaning to eat up; other sources suggest this refers to the fondness of pigs for Beechnuts.

Tastes change, however, and Beech mast has largely been recognised as a famine food. Evelyn said mast fed the poor but warned against eating the nuts raw:

> We must not omit to praise the mast, which fats our swine and deer, and hath in some families even supported men with bread. But one has to be careful with them, for they are toxic to some people.

The 17th-century scholar Abraham Munting wrote:

> In our regions this tree was only grown for its fruit, which is still being used as a source of food for the poor, as in the times of our forefathers, before they knew about grain and the baking of bread.

The consensus is that Beech nuts are edible but should not be eaten raw in large quantities because of their potential for toxicity. Despite warnings about their poisonous properties, the nuts have been used as a coffee substitute in Europe. As with anything, perhaps moderation is key. Roy Vickery reports on personal accounts of people eating Beech nuts in Dorset, England, in the 20th century:

> [During my childhood over sixty years ago, at Wimborne St Giles, Dorset] we ate Beech nuts in small quantities, but as there was a grove of Sweet Chestnuts in a field, we preferred these.
>
> — SIDMOUTH, DEVON, OCTOBER 1991

Beech nuts can be eaten raw or roasted and salted; roasting gets rid of their bitter taste. In addition, the nuts are a source of protein, magnesium, calcium, phosphorus and potassium. The seeds can also be roasted and are reportedly rich in plant starches.

It is worth remembering that Beech trees usually only fruit every three or four years, and each tree produces a pretty large quantity of mast.

Interestingly, from an American point of view, Beech nuts were seen as a sweet, delicious delicacy of the forests.

A few generations ago in central Maine, and presumably elsewhere, the gathering of Beech nuts was a regularly awaited event of October, the boys watching anxiously for the clear, cold night which presaged a black frost. Then all was bustle to catch the abundant harvest of nuts which fell from the opening burs. The nut, readily opened by the thumb-nail, is one of the northern forests' sweetest, most delicious products.

As a popular wild edible treat, American Beech nuts may be adapted for traditional dishes, such as Beech nut pie instead of pecan pie, suggests Thomas Elias and Peter Dykeman:

> For Beech nut pie, substitute 1 ½ cups Beech nuts for pecans in a pecan pie recipe.

Thus, the Americans were not deterred by the Beech nut's potential toxicity and enjoyed these wild treats of the American Beech. Arthur Haines sensibly commented on the customary gathering of *F. grandifolia* nuts:

> Consumption of large amounts of nuts could cause kidney, respiratory, and other disorders, but it would take large amounts eaten at high frequency for such disorders to occur.

He recommended roasting the nuts to reduce the alkaloid toxic saponin compound, called Fagin, to reduce the risk of such poisoning. American foragers perhaps knew better how to eat their Beech nuts than Europeans. The fruits of the American Beech have long been eaten by Native American tribes, including the Algonquin, Chippewa, Iroquois, Menominee, Ojibwa and Potawatomi.

Beech nut oil has not attracted as much attention in the US as in Europe; it is produced from many Beech species, but here we return to *F. sylvatica*. As mentioned in many authoritative texts, the pressed oil from Beech nuts is sold commercially as a frying and salad oil, heating oil, and soap manufacture. It is said to be similar to olive oil and is rich in fats and proteins.

However, the oil was so popular in France that people harvested more than two million bushels of nuts in some districts. Beech nut oil can also be made into Beech nut butter; the Silesians (people living in a historical region dividing Poland, Germany and the Czech Republic) once used it as a substitute for butter.

My friend and wild food historian, Marcus Harrison, says this about Beech oil:

> Back at the beginning of the eighteenth century, a British gentleman believed we could pay off the national debt by extracting the oil from the nut. He worked out that there were enough bushels of unused Beech masts in a 50 square mile area around London to make our own oil and stop importing from France or Germany. At that stage, Beech mast oil was a commodity. It was used for lighting and also as cooking oil. In addition, it was thought to have a better keeping quality than olive oil.

Beech mast is sometimes used as fodder for deer, pigs, and poultry. However, Gerard, too suggested the mast was primarily for animal consumption:

> [Beech nuts] with these mice and squirrels be greatly delighted, who do mightily increase by feeding thereon; swine also be fattened herewith, and certaine other beasts; also deere doe feed thereon very greedily. They be likewise pleasant to thrushes and pigeons.

From the nuts to the leaves, Beech leaves were gathered and eaten by school children in the English countryside as recently as the

20th century. You can add the leaves to salads. Mabey suggests that Beech leaves are tempting to adults as well:

> They shine in the sun from the light passing through them. To touch, they are silky and tear like delicately thin rubber. It is difficult not to want to chew a few as you walk through a Beech wood in spring. And, fresh from the tree, they are indeed a fine salad vegetable, as sweet as a mild cabbage though much softer in texture.

An old English or French recipe for Beech leaf liquor called Noyau, involves gathering the young leaves in spring to macerate in a jar of gin. According to the recipe, the liquid is then strained and mixed with hot water, sugar or honey, and other ingredients. This potent Beech drink originated in the Chilterns, England, in the 18th–19th centuries. Woodlanders managed extensive Beech woods for the chair-making industry at that time, and therefore an abundance of leaves was available to steep in gin.

Grieve tells us that although she doesn't distinguish between the first or second World War, the Germans used Beech leaves as a substitute for tobacco; the idea was not popular with their armed forces.

Various ingenious methods of harvesting the Beech as a food source have been found – often in desperate times. For example, the sawdust of Beech once provided an emergency bulking agent for flour in bread baked by European peasants. In Norway and pre-industrial Sweden (particularly in times of crop failure), the sawdust was boiled in water, baked and then mixed with flour to make the bread. In addition, Beech wood may have provided the fuel for bakers' ovens because it burned fast and hot.

In the Balkans, Beech material was macerated in cold water, and the liquid was added to milk as a starter culture for making yoghurt. The flower buds were eaten as a raw snack or cooked in vegetable dishes in the Czech Republic. In Bosnia-Herzegovina, the young leaves, nuts and bark were used as a 'mush' to make bread. In Poland, the nuts were once eaten as a children's snack, roasted in the oven, pressed to produce oil and used as a coffee substitute. The leaf buds were eaten raw. Such uses gradually declined in the 20th century.

Beech wood is said to be one of the best woods for smoking foods. In Germany, it is used to smoke a beer called Bamberger Rauchbier; in Spain, it smokes a sheep's cheese called Idiazabal. In addition, chips from the wood have been used to age beer.

As we have discussed, the American Beech tree (*F. grandifolia*) provides similar food stuffs such as edible nuts that can be roasted, ground for flour, used as a coffee substitute or pressed for oil. The young shoots too can be cooked.

Germinating seeds are a crisp, sweet and nutty-flavoured snack. Around the world, different species of Beech have inspired similar cooking traditions. In addition, Beech trees are used as condiments, spice, or flavours, such as the leaves and seeds of *F. avicennae* and *F. budrunga* in southeast Asia.

In Africa, the seeds of *F. inaequalis* provide a cooking oil. In Japan, the seeds of *F. crenata* are roasted and give an oil. In Thailand, various Beeches are harvested for their young shoots. In Asia, *F. tataricum* seeds are ground to make flour. In Punjab, India, *F. jacquemontii* twigs were eaten raw or as a chutney.

Roasted Beech Nuts

Evenly spread Beech nuts on a baking tray, then bake for 5 minutes at 100ºC, 250ºF.

Aged Beech Leaf Tea

In Autumn or Winter, pick a decent amount of aged, honey-golden Beech leaves from a tree or hedge. Put 5 grams of leaves into a teapot and add 500ml of boiling water. Allow the brew to infuse for 15 minutes, then serve. The flavours are reminiscent of a Japanese ryokucha or sencha tea.

Beech Nut Toffee

Add 500 grams of sugar and 10 ml of water to a heavy-bottomed saucepan. Stir over low heat until the sugar is slightly browned and very thick. Next, mix in 500g of chopped Beech nuts. Pour into a flat buttered dish and allow to cool before slicing into squares.

MEDICINE

Healers used the magical powers of the Beech in early healing rituals to drive away harm from a person or ensure a good outcome for the patient. For example, cold spa water poured nine times over Beech ash, mixed with linseed oil, was an old remedy for burns and painful wounds. Likewise, beach tea mixed with pig's lard was believed to relieve the symptoms of rheumatism.

Pregnant women needed to use Beech wood with caution. A very ancient belief told that Beech wood brought into the house would make labour more painful and possibly cause the child's death. Gerard wrote:

> [The Beech] being brought into the house there follows hard travail of child, and miserable deaths.

In Germany, people thought that a pregnant woman who drank a decoction made from the wood of the so-called Miracle Beech, near Bavaria, would give birth to a boy, whereas a decoction of lime wood would produce a girl. Providing the child survived all this meddling before they were even born, Beech leaves were then used to stuff mattresses in the belief that it would help the child grow.

As an aside, Beech leaf mattresses were supposedly very comfortable and long-lasting. They were called Lits de Parlement in France, or talking beds, because the soft, fragrant leaves were said to rustle musically or crackle incessantly, depending on your point of view.

Ancient healers knew how to use Beech for medicine as well as magic. For example, Pliny recommended Beech leaves for infected gums and lips. Indeed, the leaves were prescribed to apply to blisters for their soothing, binding effects.

The renowned German abbess Hildegard of Bingen included Beech as an ingredient in a recipe to cure jaundice. A later herbal from the 15th century provided a recipe for deafness using beach leaves:

> Take the juice of leaves of a Beech-tree, and good vinegar, even portions, and put thereto powder of quick-lime; and then clear it through a cloth; and of this, when it is cleansed, put hot into the sick ear.

Gerard suggested Beech nuts, or mast, were helpful for kidney and urinary stones:

> The kernels or mast within are reported to ease the paine of the kidnies proceeding of the stone if they be eaten, and to cause the gravell and sand the easier to come forth.

His contemporary, the Flemish herbalist Rembert Dodoens (1517–1585), better known as Dodonaeus, valued Beech nuts as medicine as the ancient Romans did:

> The kernels of the Beech nuts (Nucus fagi) are sweet. They are useful for expelling the gravel and broken (kidney) stones together with the urine.

The English herbalist Nicholas Culpeper (1616–1654) placed the Beech under the dominion of Saturn with the influence of this planet upon its properties:

> The leaves of the Beech tree are cooling and binding, and therefore good to be applied to hot swellings to discuss them; the nuts do much nourish such beasts as feed thereon. The water that is found in the hollow places of decaying Beeches will cure both man and beast of scurf, or running tetters, if they be washed therewith; you may boil the leaves into poultice, or make an ointment of them when time of year serves.

Following the recommendations of Gerard, Dodonaeus and Culpeper, healers added the ash of Beech to an ointment for bladder stones. A mixture of honey and Beech ash was a remedy for scabies. In Gloucestershire, England, people took an infusion of Beech buds to treat boils and piles.

As Culpeper mentioned, when you collected water in the hollow of a Beech tree, it was believed to have healing properties. English writer and gardener John Evelyn (1620–1706) wrote:

> [It cures] the most obstinate tetters, scabs, and scurfs, in man or beast, fomenting the part with it.

A report from the Devonshire Association in 1971 also claimed that it cured baldness.

Around the world, different Beech species have been used in folk medicine. In North America, for example, the Cherokee chewed the nuts of the native American Beech (*F. grandifolia*) to get rid of worm infestations. In addition, the tree's inner bark has been used as an antiseptic decoction for cleansing and skin complaints by the Iroquois, Malecite and Rappahannock tribes.

In present-day herbalism, Beech bark is considered an astringent thanks to its rich plant tannins, and it's thought to have fever-fighting properties. In addition, the bark of younger branches can be prepared as a laxative or to expel worms; de Cleene and Lejeune warn that it may cause nausea if overused.

The leaves have a diuretic effect, and herbalists use them for kidney problems. A decoction of the bark or leaves similarly may be helpful for bladder, kidney and liver problems, just as herbalists wrote centuries ago. In addition, a decoction of the roots or leaves has been recommended for fevers, dysentery or diabetes.

Beech oil and tar have been used for skin complaints and chest infections because of the antiseptic and expectorant effects. In Kentucky, US, Beech syrup was used as a treatment for tuberculosis. Creosote made from Beech tar was used to relieve the pain of toothache due to its analgesic and antiseptic properties and replace phenol in some soaps because it's considered a good skin disinfectant. Charcoal, called Carbo Ligni Depuratus, from Beech, was believed to alleviate phosphorus and alkaline poisoning.

In North America, the American Beech is used similarly to heal burns and scalds for chest infections and heart problems. The nuts are chewed for worms, and the tree also provides a wash to alleviate the rash of poison ivy.

In subtle medicine traditions, interested in harmonising emotions and bringing balance to the body's energies, Beech flower remedy is recommended for those who "feel the need to see more good and beauty in all that surrounds them".

In scientific research, Pujol and team (2016) discovered the antiviral potential of the European Beech (*F. sylvatica*) against the herpes virus. The authors concluded that the tree contains promising compounds that may have "various applications in pharmacy", particularly against the herpes virus, as well as some mode of action against polio and dengue viruses. The Beech's antiviral compounds work by inhibiting the cells of the viruses.

SAFETY NOTE

Beech nuts contain trimethylamine and possibly other saponins, so best to avoid raw as they can damage the mucus membrane in the intestinal tract. Always cook or roast Beech nuts.

Severe poisoning incidents are known, which are suspected of having been the result of the victim eating fewer than fifty Beech nuts.

Duke writes the American Beech (*F. americana*) is dangerous in pregnancy and may cause miscarriage. However, I would caution the same for the Common or European Beech (*Fagus sylvatica*) due to the reasons above.

BLACKTHORN (SLOE)
Prunus spinosa

FAMILY

Rosaceae.

BOTANICAL DESCRIPTION

Height: small tree or shrub growing up to 4 m tall. Flowers: snowy-white flowers. Stems: black, leafless stems. Bark: blackish bark. Twigs: many branched spiny stems. Leaves: oval-like leaves. Fruit: dark purplish berries. Foliage: impenetrable thicket of thorny branches.

FLOWERS

March to May.

STATUS

Perennial. Native.

HABITAT

Deciduous woodland, hedgerows, river banks, scrub.

OVERVIEW

The Blackthorn in blossom must be one of the few harbingers of spring that is unwelcome after a long, hard winter.

The snowy-white flowers of the Blackthorn against its striking, black, leafless stems provide a lovely, early springtime sight, inspiring one of its names, 'the lady of pearls'. - Gabrielle Hatfield

While the beautiful blossoms were a symbol of feminine beauty, the tree's tough wood, sharp thorns and bitter fruits were believed to house an evil presence.

Indeed, few shrubs as unlucky as Blackthorn and its formidable reputation darkly reverberate through folk history.

FOOD

There appear to be few uses for Blackthorn in the kitchen. Instead, foragers look for sloe berries to gather from September to November and the bitter fruit for making sloe gin. The Welsh poem Cad Godeu suggests that sloes can only be enjoyed by children who get a thrill from the bitter taste: "The Blackthorn full of spines – how the child delights in its fruit".

It seems our ancestors had a taste for bitter foods too. There is some evidence at a Neolithic site in northern Italy that the fruits were cooked or roasted.

Picking sloes, sometimes called slaes or sloans, in late autumn is a well-kept countryside tradition. In the 1700s, Robert Bloomfield described roasting sloes over a bonfire in The Farmer's Boy, and in the 1900s, Victorian writer Anne Pratt recalled collecting sloes as a child and burying the fruit in a bottle until winter to make a preserve.

If you were brave, the ripe fruits could be eaten raw after "having been mellowed by frost". In France, the unripe fruits are pickled like olives. In Azerbaijan, the ripe fruits are pickled with onions and garlic. Dried sloes can also add flavour to herbal teas.

Sloe wine has been made for hundreds of years, and the bitter-tasting fruits are still used to make sloe gin, flavour liqueurs, and even added to ice cream. Sloe gin is drunk as an after-dinner winter drink because of its warming qualities. You can also make the dark berries into jellies and jams (in Ireland); sloes and Crab Apples make a delicious jelly.

While you may find many recipes online to make sloe gin, experienced foragers will tell you the best time to pick the fruits is after the first frost. This makes sure the skins are soft and better for mixing with gin. Sloe gin is a slow process but worth the wait with an additional treat of gin sOaked berries at the end.

For an alternative boozy liquor chocolate, try pureeing through a sieve and then mixing the fruit pulp into melted chocolate. Cool and serve.

In ancient Ireland, sloes could have been an emergency food in times of famine. The fresh fruits are strongly astringent and might have been eaten dried then rehydrated to taste more like stewed plums. Sloe stones have been uncovered in excavations of Viking Dublin dating back 1,000 years. The fruit can also be fermented into fruit vinegar.

In County Roscommon, Ireland, a Halloween custom was to bake a cake and put inside a ring, a coin, a chip of wood, and a sloe. Whoever got the coin would be rich, and whoever got the ring would be married first. Whoever got the chip of wood would be the first to die, and whoever got the sloe would live the longest. The reasoning behind the sloe's gift was because the fairies blighted the sloes and other berries in November; thus it was likely to be the last edible sloe of the year. The tradition survives today in Ireland with a fruit loaf made at Halloween containing a ring.

Sloes have been gathered in many Mediterranean countries to eat as fruit or to make traditional dishes. In Spain, Portugal, Italy, Slovenia and Turkey, sloes were picked straight from the tree and eaten ripe in autumn or overripe after the first frost.

In Spain, the fruits were used to make a Christmas dessert and in southern parts, cooks mixed boiled sloes with wine. In the Basque Navarra region, sloes were sOaked in anisette (an anise-flavoured liqueur) with coffee beans, cinnamon or vanilla pods and drunk as a digestif called patxaran or pacharán.

In Catalonia, sloes were mixed with other herbs to make flavoured liqueurs taken for medicinal purposes and enjoyment. In Italy and Bosnia-Herzegovina, Blackthorn leaves were used as a substitute for tobacco.

Blackthorn may be an ancestor of other fruit trees such as plum and greengage. The idea that plums might be related to Blackthorn is reflected in the Life of Brigid. The saint blessed an alder tree to bear two-thirds apples and one-third sloes, which tasted sweet rather than sour. It has been suggested the saint's power had either sweetened the fruit or that the story refers to an early plum descendant of Blackthorn. John Wiersema and Blanca León record Blackthorn as a "crop relative for Japanese plum".

Whatever it's claim to ancestry, Blackthorn fruits score well in nutritional tables. On average, fresh sloes contain about 10 mg of vitamin C and 5 mg of vitamin E per 100 g. They are rich in other nutrients with an impressive 453 mg potassium, 5 mg calcium and 22 mg magnesium per 100 g. They are very high in antioxidant compounds, phenols and flavonoids, and essential fatty acids, which are thought to bring many health benefits, such as reducing the incidence of chronic disease.

An unusual use of the fruit is for making fruit leathers. Sloes are collected and crushed into a paste and thinly spread on bark to dry. The method reduces the astringency in the fruit and preserves it for storage over winter. In addition, if the leather was heated, it released fruit sugars and made the dried sloes sweeter to eat.

In Transylvania, Blackthorn juice and seeds are used with stomach rennet to curdle milk.

The flowers can be eaten and crystallised or sugared, and the leaves can make tea. However, a scandalous use of Blackthorn leaves in Victorian times was as an adulterant of tea. CP Johnson said that four million pounds of Blackthorn leaves were packaged up in a fraudulent attempt to sell them off as genuine China tea at one time. Rascals.

In 1995 the Irish Folklore Commission documented the use of dried Blackthorn leaves, called Irish tea, as a tobacco substitute.

Traditional Sloe Gin

- 300g sloes (frozen)
- 1-litre gin
- 4tbsp of sugar

Take your frozen sloes and crush them with a rolling pin until smashed up, then transfer them to a Kilner jar. Add the sugar, and pour in the gin. Shake vigorously and leave for a minimum of 3 months, but best if left for a year. Shake occasionally when you remember. Check the taste and if you feel like it, add more sugar if you think it needs it. But really, this is a different sloe gin recipe to the one you are primarily used to - strain and bottle for later use.

...ow Jam

- ...sehips
- ...loes
- ...Crab Apples
- 300g blackberries & raspberries
- 300g sugar

Wash and clean the fruit. Put the rosehips, sloes and chopped Crab Apples into a preserving pan. Add water to cover and simmer until all the fruits are tender. Pass the fruit mixture through a jam strainer. Keep the liquid, weigh it and pour into a large saucepan. Add the same amount of sugar as there is liquid, then add the blackberries, raspberries and simmer for 15 minutes, or until the mixture reaches the setting point. Pour into sterilised jars and put lids on immediately. Makes 10 small jars.

MEDICINE

Blackthorn was used in transference charms. It worked by employing sympathetic magic – transferring a person's illness into itself or another object or living thing. For example, cattle doctors in Worcestershire treated footrot by cutting a sod of earth from where the animal had trod and then hanging the turf on the tree as the soil dried out, so the animal would be healed.

Healers used the slight acidity of its fruit to burn off warts. A sloe was rubbed on the wart and thrown over the shoulder. Another way to remove warts was to rub a black snail on the skin and then impale the poor creature on the tree's thorns. The wart would vanish as the snail perished. The use of Blackthorn for warts in British folk medicine was largely restricted to parts of southern England.

Early herbalists documented several uses for Blackthorn, particularly for stemming the flow of blood in the body caused by an ailment or wound. John Gerard (1545–1612)wrote in 1597 that sloe juice could:

> Stop the belly, the laske and the bloody flixe, the inordinate course of womens termes, and all other issues of blood in man or woman.

To which Nicholas Culpeper (1616–1654) agreed:

> All the parts of the Sloe-Bush are binding, cooling, and dry, and all effectual to stay bleeding at the nose and mouth, or any other place; the lask of the belly or stomach, or the bloody flux, the too much abounding of women's courses, and helps to ease the pains of the sides, and bowels.

Culpeper approved of the tree as a digestive tonic that could: "ease all manner of gnawings in the stomach, the sides and bowels, or any griping pains in any of them".

The astringent berries and bark have been used to prevent diarrhoea, and in the Scottish Highlands, the flowers made into a laxative; an infusion of the thorns treated diarrhoea in Ireland; the thorns were said to treat diarrhoea in animals, as well as people, well into the 20th century in Britain and Ireland.

In Ireland, the leaves were a remedy for indigestion and summer fever. According to a Welsh belief, if you ate the first three Blackthorn blossoms that you saw, you would be relieved from heartburn all year round.

In Ireland, sloe gin was once thought to be good for the kidneys and is used to treat colic in babies and worms in children.

Some sources say Irish herbalists disliked sloes because they are too astringent. However, in parts of Britain and Ireland, healers valued the astringent quality of sloes for treating coughs and colds. In North Wales, sloes were a treatment for coughs. In the Scottish Highlands, sloe jelly was good for the throat, and in East Anglia, people gargled sloe juice for a sore throat. Sucking sloes was also said to cure painful gum boils. Traditionally, the leaves made an excellent gargle to ease swellings in the throat and mouth.

A gipsy remedy for bronchitis used peeled bark boiled in water, cooled, and added to drink. Healers made the inner bark into a tea to treat several conditions in Sussex.

Blackthorn was considered to be a cooling, drying herb in the older system of medicine. Thus, bathing the forehead or temples in an infusion of the leaves or flowers would relieve pains of the head.

Sloes have long been valued in the Mediterranean for their astringent properties. Sloe liqueurs were drunk to prevent or relieve digestive problems. The raw fruits were eaten to treat diarrhoea, and the overripe fruits were taken as a laxative.

In present-day herbalism, the tree is a potential treatment for many ailments and diseases. Its astringent, diuretic, laxative and purgative properties make Blackthorn the tree of choice for treating: inflammation, rheumatism, gout, water retention, constipation, diarrhoea, dysentery and intestinal worms. It is also helpful for asthma, colds, headaches and nausea. In addition, it is listed as a herbal aid for childbirth and nausea and for treating colic in babies.

Many of the traditional uses of Blackthorn in herbal medicine survive. For example, a syrup of sloes is given as an astringent medicine used to stem nose bleeding, just as it was in Culpeper's time. In addition, sloe syrup is good for dental health, being massaged on to gums to prevent tooth loss or rubbed on to teeth to clean and whiten; an infusion of the leaves can be used as a cleansing and whitening mouth wash.

A valuable herb to have in the bathroom cabinet, Blackthorn can be used as a cosmetic lotion for cleansing skin and banishing blemishes. In addition, its fruits are used as a base for vaginal rinses, stomach complaints, and diarrhoea, and a decoction of its bark to treat fever.

Blackthorn belongs to a group of plants that contain cyanide-producing compounds which "stimulates respiration, improves digestion and gives a sense of wellbeing".

Gironés-Vilaplana and team (2013) studied the benefits of health drinks made with lemon juice and berries, including Blackthorn fruit. The result was a reportedly pleasant drink of an attractive colour with significantly high antioxidant values.

Wolbiś and team (2001) studied the chemical components, such as triterpenes and plant sterols, in the flowers and leaves of Blackthorn. They found the flowers contain anti-inflammatory ursolic and oleanolic acids.

SAFETY NOTE

Little research is available on the plant's toxicity, but it appears that the thorns inflict the most damage. Yewlett and team (2009) investigated the case of a patient injured by an embedded thorn of Blackthorn, which had caused inflamed tendons.

Tiong and Butt (2009) investigated a penetrating Blackthorn injury to the wrist, which they reported is common in rural communities due to farming or gardening activities. They found that the thorns, often contaminated with soil, caused numerous tissue reactions once embedded under the skin.

Sharma and Meredith (2004) reviewed a report of 18 Blackthorn injuries of upper limbs and recommended anyone with a Blackthorn injury should have immediate medical treatment to avoid further complications. The authors concluded that most patients were male and the majority injured between March and August or during the hedge-cutting time.

One hopes the sight of Blackthorn blossom along hedgerows in spring will remain a familiar sight and that the habit of picking sloes in autumn will remain a countryside habit. Beware the Blackthorn's sharp branches, however, for they are far worse than a Blackthorn winter.

So far, studies have not raised concerns about using Blackthorn as a medicinal herb during pregnancy, while breastfeeding or when taking other medications. However, caution is always advised, and if in doubt, then avoid using the herb at these times and consult your health practitioner for more information.

James Duke, in his Handbook of Medicinal Herbs, suggests Blackthorn should not be used long-term. He mentions cyanide-related compounds in the plant, although the potential side effects of therapeutic dosages of Blackthorn are not known.

CRAB APPLE
Malus sylvestris

FAMILY

Rosaceae.

BOTANICAL DESCRIPTION

Height: a small and spiny tree or shrub rarely reaching a great height. Leaves: dark green and glossy. Buds and flowers: buds are deep-tinged with pink on the outside; the flowers appear as small clusters, pink and white, and attract many bees. Fruit: small, round yellow apples, sometimes red.

FLOWERS

April to May.

STATUS

Perennial. Native.

HABITAT

Deciduous woodland, hedgerows, scrub.

OVERVIEW

> *The crab of the wood is sauce very good for the crab of the sea,*
> *But the wood of the crab is sauce for a drab that will not her husband obey.*
>
> — TF THISELTON DYER (1889)

The awkward cousin of the cultivated apple, Crab Apple (*Malus sylvestris*) is sometimes credited as the ancestor of all apples. However, its value as a fruit-producing tree is often overlooked because of the unattractive, crabby appearance of its small, hard fruit. But the discovery of Crab Apple remnants in Neolithic Oak coffins in Denmark suggest that the tree has been a source of food, or ritual, since ancient times.

John E Bryan and Coralie Castle wrote in The Edible Ornamental Garden:

> "It is estimated that 2000 varieties of apple are now grown, mostly in cooler climates where they reach perfection. The apple does not come true from seed, though, so that while there were many thousands of seedlings sown and grown, the modern production of apples came to the fore only when selections were made and the best varieties were propagated asexually or by vegetative means. Crab Apple trees are selected more for their shape, colourful flowers or decorative fruit, than their prodigious harvest, though it is possible to have a good crop."

A small tree or shrub of hedges and woodlands, Crab Apple, grows wild in many parts of Britain and Europe. The Crab Apple tree has narrow, oval green leaves, and it provides small, white fragrant blossoms in spring and yields small, round red or yellow fruit. In Gaelic, Crab Apple was called abhall. Malus means 'apple tree', and sylvestris means' wild' or 'undomesticated', being of the woods.

The root of the word 'apple' is the same in Celtic and Slavonian languages; this suggests that the tree was introduced to Britain, although Crab Apple is described as a native of lowland Britain in many texts. Ap means in Zend and Sanskrit' water', and p'hala means 'fruit', thus the name meant 'juicy fruit'. Pomum, Latin for apple, is derived from potare, drink, and poculum, a cup.

FOOD

Mrs Grieve tells us that apple cooking is one of the earliest inclinations among children who love apples cooked and uncooked and the homeliness of apple pie and apple puddings. On this topic, the old tradition of apple pudding is well recorded:

> "In Shakespeare's time, apples when served at dessert were usually accompanied by caraway, as we may read in Henry IV, where Shallow invites Falstaff to 'a pippin and a dish of caraway,' In a still earlier Booke of Nurture' it is directed 'After mete pepyns, caraway in comfyts.' The custom of serving roast apples with a little saucerful of Carraways is still kept up at Trinity College, Cambridge, and at some of the old-fashioned London Livery dinners, just as in Shakespeare's days".

Mrs Grieve wrote in A Modern Herbal about Crab Apple:

> "It has a very austere and acid juice, in consequence of which it cannot be eaten in the raw condition, but a delicious jelly is made from it, which is always welcome on the table, and the fruit can also be used for jam-making, with blackberries, pears or quinces."

Despite its sour taste, Crab Apple has made a surprising contribution to apple cookery. Many find Crab Apple jelly, or Crab Apple and blackberry jelly, or Crab Apple wine to be pleasing, and a couple of Crab Apples in an apple tart can improve its flavour. Crab Apple is relatively high in pectin and is also added to ensure jams and jellies are set. For example, it is beneficial for jams made with low pectin fruit such as strawberries. In addition, you can mix Crab Apple with other wild fruits to make jellies such as Rowanberries, rosehips, Hawthorn and sloes. Richard Mabey suggests that Crab Apple makes a good hedgerow jam with blackberry, elderberry, wild plum, and Hazelnuts as good companions. Gabrielle Hatfield writes:

> "As a foodstuff, Crab Apples were invaluable and there is no shortage of recipes, for wine for example or for an excellent jelly to accompany meat or to eat as a jam. In the past, where grain was scarce, crab-apple pulp was dried and mixed with flour for bread-making."

Crab Apple also makes pleasant fruit cheeses mixed with blackberries or other fruits. Fruit cheeses are like a stiff jelly that can be cut into slices and eaten with roast duck, goose or game. It is recommended to pickle Crab Apples in spiced vinegar and serve with pork. Other uses for these sour fruit are for making syrup, apple butter, spiced apples and wine. Many foragers of wild edibles also suggest that the aromatic flavour of Crab Apples is especially good after first frost, which reduces its tart taste.

While some suggest Crab Apples are generally an unloved fruit, there is potential to put them to good use in the kitchen. Sara Bir writes:

> "There are hundreds of varieties of Crab Apples, and many of them are useless in culinary terms-tiny, hard as pellets, and unrelentingly tanic. But a resourceful person who finds a tree bearing Crab Apples that are larger and juicier will, come fall, never be bored. Hours and hours of picking and goofy kitchen experimentation await."

While Crab Apples may not be the most popular variety of apples, one can assume that you can use the fruit in place of cultivated apples in recipes. Thus, the use of Crab Apples in the kitchen is endless. Overall, you can use Crab Apples in cooking much as any apple - sliced, chopped, grated, and so on. Some examples include as an addition to cheese platters, chutneys, dips, fillers for sandwiches, crepes, tarts, pies. In addition, Crab Apples can be cored and roasted with pork or goose and baked and served with lots of sugar and cream.

If you do make an apple pie with Crab Apples, don't forget these two English rhymes that govern apple-pie making:

If old Christmas Day be fair and bright
Ye'd have apples to your heart's delight.

Till St Swithin's day be past
The apples be not fit to taste.

People once brewed Crab Apple tea by slicing the apples, simmering for an hour, and mixing with honey. You can make a pleasant tea from the leaves. The fully ripe fruit can be dried to make tea or harvested after first frost to juice; other possible uses for apple juice is as an ingredient for lemonade, fruit wine, punch, chutney, pudding sauce, compotes, sorbets and fruit casserole.

Verjuice, made from crushed Crab Apples, is sometimes described as a 'cider' or 'vinegar', which can be used as a substitute for lemon juice when strained and left for a month. Verjuice has been used by cooks since Medieval times and was popular in Britain until the nineteenth century. It is still a popular ingredient in France. In Ireland, verjuice is used as a lemon juice substitute in jellies, wines and cider, and, combined with blackberry, a mousse and pudding. It was also once used to curdle milk.

There are many traditional drinks associated with apples and in particular Crab Apples. Peter Jackson writes that cider-making was less a traditional activity in Ireland than in Britain. Still, until recent times, County Limerick and County Clare had a strong history of cider-making. In Clonmel, County Tipperary is the home of Bulmers Cider (sold as Magners Cider overseas) since 1935. Mrs Grieve adds, "In Ireland, it [Crab Apple] is sometimes added to cider, to impart a roughness."

Crab Apples can also be roasted and added to the wassail bowl, a traditional Christmas Eve beverage. Other traditional drinks are associated with Crab Apple. For example, "A drink called wherry in Yorkshire used to be made from the pulp after the verjuice had been expressed." In England, at Halloween, a hot spiced ale, wine or cider with apples and bits of toast in it was drunk, called Lamb's Wool, which comes from the Irish Apple Gathering Day. Donald Watts writes: "Even without the ale; roasted crabs were a favourite fruit in days gone by…though nobody would take the trouble to cook them these days."

In parts of Europe, Crab Apples were useful wild edibles in times of scarcity. They are listed as a winter fruit for picking and storage, by freezing, in Estonia and pre-industrial Sweden. In Sarajevo, people made a beverage from pickled wild fruits including *M. sylvestris*. In Gorbeialdea (Bicay, Basque Country), Crab Apple is one of seven wild edible plants traditionally gathered to make liquors and a traditional cider called pitikin.

You can also use other parts of the Crab Apple tree in the kitchen. For example, the flowers can be crystallised and used as cake or biscuit decorations. Treat them as elderflowers by deep frying and sprinkling with sugar or adding to fritter batter.

The young, tart, fruity leaves can be picked in spring, added to mixed herbs, put into sauces, and dried as a tea.

An edible oil can be obtained from Crab Apple seeds. However, this is not commercially viable unless produced in larger quantities as a side product to harvesting the Crab Apples - such as Crab Apple cider, where you could extract the seeds from the leftover apple pulp.

Nutritionally, most apples contain a high percentage of water, from 80 to 85 per cent, and the remaining 10 to 15 per cent being starches and sugars and various other constituents.

Despite their high water content, apples are rich in vitamins. They are classed as an essential anti-scorbutic fruit for relieving scurvy and containing organic acids, malic acid, gallic acid, and various salts of potash, soda, lime, magnesium, and iron.

Grieve wrote that it should be unpeeled to get the full benefit of eating an apple, although it is uncertain whether this applies to cultivated and wild apples. Few studies describe the nutritional content of Crab Apples.

Verjuice of Crab-Apples

In October, take crap apples and juice them using a juicer. Alternatively, puree the Crab Apples in a food processor and then strain through muslin overnight by placing a heavyweight on top to extract as much juice as possible. I use a 10kg kettlebell. Put the liquid into a jar and leave open for about a week or until the juice develops a sour taste, then cap and keep in the refrigerator. Use instead of lemon juice or vinegar.

Crab Apple Jelly

Put the cleaned Crab Apples into a pan and cover them with cold water. Bring to a boil, then simmer until the fruit starts breaking up into a pulp. Pour through a jelly bag and leave overnight. Measure out the liquid and for every 500 ml, add 450g of sugar to a preserving pan. Heat until the sugar has melted, then rapidly boil for 20 to 30 minutes until stiff. Put into jars, cap and store.

Spiced Crab Apples

Wash and halve the ¾ kilo of Crab Apples, then put them into cold water to prevent them from going brown. Do not core. Heat 500 ml of cider vinegar and 750 g of sugar until the sugar has dissolved, then add the Crab Apples along with ½ tsp ground ginger, ¼ tsp ground cloves and 1 tsp of ground cinnamon. Simmer until the apples are tender. You do not want them to start breaking up. Using a slotted spoon, lift them out and put them into warmed jars. Next, boil the remaining syrup until reduced by half and pour over the Crab Apples. Seal when cold and store in a dark place. Allow them to infuse for two months before using them.

MEDICINE

People often used the apple tree in magical healing. Like many other trees that feature in folklore, it was believed to absorb diseases such as fever, gout, and toothache to get better. Minor ailments like verrucas and corns would disappear, for example, if the afflicted person rubbed them with cut apples, then put the pieces of the fruit back together and hid them. Other diseases were thought possible to transfer to apples, such as smallpox. In Norfolk, an apple was left in the sufferer's room where the fruit would become spotty, and the patient would recover. Eating an apple studded with peppercorns was meant to relieve fever. Peeling an apple in an upward direction would prevent vomiting, and peeling an apple in a downward direction would prevent diarrhoea.

In official medicine, apples have been used in countless ways for centuries. Classical physician Dioscorides (c50 AD) recommended apples as a laxative and eradicate worms. Italian herbalist Matthiolus (c1500–1577) attributed apple juice to the same effects and said it eased the pain of a stitch in the side. In folk medicine, a widespread use was pureed apple added to lard to make an ointment for cracked skin. Such creams were called pommata, from which comes the word pomade. Apples were also a common home remedy for headaches.

Mrs Grieve wrote about the beneficial effects of the refreshing smell of apples:

> "The peculiar winy odour is stimulating to many. Pliny, and later, Sir John Mandeville, tell of a race of little men in 'Farther India' who 'eat naught and live by the smell of apples.' Burton wrote that apples are good against melancholy and Dr. John Caius, physician to Queen Elizabeth, in his Boke of Counseille against the Sweatynge Sicknesse advises the patient to 'smele to an old swete apple to recover his strengthe.' An apple stuck full of cloves was the prototype of the pomander, and pomatum (now used only in a general sense) took its name from being first made of the pulp of apples, lard and rosewater."

While none of these remedies described above refers specifically to Crab Apples, we may assume that the wild fruit shared some of the qualities and uses of cultivated apple trees and apples in folk medicine. Yet, on the whole, people largely ignored Crab Apples in folk medicine in favour of the cultivated variety. For example, John Pechey (1694) recommended apples to treat melancholy and fevers; the favoured type was fragrant pippins. Rotten apples were even applied as a poultice to sore eyes.

While people preferred cultivated apples in folk medicine, the Crab Apple was valued as a potent magic drink called verjuice. Healers used this magical brew to heal bruises and sprains and burns, scalds, or inflammation. In other testimonies, Coles described:

"The juice of Crabs, which we commonly call Verjuice, applyed with wet cloathes to such places as are burned and scalded, cooleth, healeth, and draweth the fire out of them".

The herbalist Gerard recommended verjuice to remove "the heat of burnings, scaldings, and all inflammations", provided you put it on early enough, it stopped, he said, any blistering. He also prescribed it for skin ailments, for it "taketh away the heat of S. Antonies fire, all inflammations whatsoever". Salmon (1693) had this to say about Crab Apples or wildlings, "They are cold and astringent, but boyled or scalded, and eaten with Butter and Sugar, they strengthen the Stomach, quench thirst, and cool the heat of Fevers."

The juice was used as a laxative; this may be related to the fact that apples were extremely well digested and beneficial for the bowels, which was discovered very early on. Thus the saying:

To eat an apple before going to bed
Will make the doctor beg his bread.

The Physicians of Myddfai used roasted Crab Apples to treat ailing infants by taking "some of the pulp, and half as much honey: let this be the child's only sustenance for a day and a night". In Irish folk medicine, people used Crab Apple mixed with buttermilk to soothe sore throats and internal cancer. In Scottish Highlands, they used Crab Apples to treat sprains and cramps.

Finally, a Bach flower remedy is made from the flowering twigs of the Crab Apple tree intended to cleanse a person who feels not quite right about themselves. Perhaps there is a link here to Grieve's assertion that the scent of apples can dispel melancholy.

Apples have long been associated with health; as the saying goes "An apple a day keeps the doctor away" while chewing a raw apple provides good exercise for the gums and teeth, and the fruit acids clean the teeth. The regular drinking of cider in Normandy was even associated with a low level of kidney stones in the population.

In modern herbal medicine, Crab Apple is a cleansing tonic used to treat stomach and bowel disorders, diarrhoea, and perhaps to a lesser extent today, to treat scabies. Eating apples is known to stimulate the digestive system and protect against constipation. The soluble fibre of the fruit helps lower cholesterol, which is good for protecting the heart and circulation. People who have gastric problems are often advised to start or end a meal with an apple.

You can make dried apple peel or apple slices into a tea to cool a fever or inflammation. De Cleene and Lejeune write, "The flesh of a fresh peeled and cored apple has been shown to be a good remedy against certain types of both acute and chronic inflammation of the intestinal mucosa, even if it is associated with severe diarrhoea or vomiting." In addition, the fresh fruit pulp can be used as a poultice to relieve inflammation or minor flesh wounds.

Apples are also still thought to be suitable for treating gout, rheumatism, and hardening of the arteries and are considered a helpful addition to the diet for people suffering from kidney and liver ailments with metabolic disorders.

The active ingredients that make apples such a healthy food are pectin and polyphenols, found mainly in the skin. Research has shown that eating an apple regularly can reduce the risk of diseases such as chronic disease (cardiovascular, diabetes, lung dysfunction and cancer). In addition, some research suggests that pectin can protect the body against radiation.

In Turkey, Azerbaijan and Iran, *M. sylvestris* has been recorded as a medicinal plant for respiratory system diseases. It is also listed as a wild medicinal herb in an ethnobotanical study in the Kopaonik

Mountain (Central Serbia). In Croatia, *M. sylvestris* is made into a homemade vinegar by the Istro-Romanian community for various medicinal uses. In the Albanian Alps, Kosovo, the fruit is extracted and mixed with sugar or made into a decoction to treat cholesterol and diabetes.

Further research into the chemistry of Crab Apple by Richardson and team (2020) found that the fruit is a source of stable vitamin C glycoside. In addition, Crab Apple leaves contain about 2.4% of an antibacterial component called florin, which can slow the growth of certain bacteria. Crab Apple bark, mainly the bark of the root, is anthelmintic, refrigerant and soporific. Some herbalists recommend an infusion to treat intermittent, remittent and bilious fevers. Mrs Grieve writes, "The bark of the Apple-tree which is bitter, especially the root-bark, contains a principle called Phloridzin, and a yellow colouring matter, Quercetin, both extracted by boiling water. The seeds give Amygdaline and edible oil."

SAFETY NOTE

Conway warns that you should not eat Crab Apples in excess because this can cause griping abdominal pains and upset; further, he says that Crab Apples cause these symptoms with ease and should never be eaten raw.

Although in meagre quantities, the fruit seeds contain hydrocyanic acid and should not be eaten in excess. However, a whole apple may be consumed entirely, as the amount of hydrocyanic acids in the seeds is very low.

DOG ROSE (ROSEHIP)
Rosa canina

FAMILY

Rosaceae.

BOTANICAL DESCRIPTION

Height: up to 10 ft. Stems: arched and thorny. Flowers: large, white or pink, five-petalled flowers. Leaves: green, oval toothed leaves. Fruit: oblong, orange-red berry bearing small, hairy fruits (or seeds) inside. Foliage: a climber with long branches and arching twigs.

FLOWERS

June to July.

STATUS

Perennial. Native.

HABITAT

Prefers heavy clay soils, seen in gardens and fields.

OVERVIEW

The rose family (Rosaceae) is a large clan of dozens of species and thousands of hybrids. It is one of the most famous flowers in the world prized for its beauty and fragrance. Rose petals are made into scented sachets, distilled into rosewater, and sold as expensive oils and perfumes.

However, the rose is not just a pretty face – it is a wild edible that you can eat from root to tip: the flowers flavour cakes, jellies, puddings, syrups and wine. The fruits, or rosehips, are added to salads, sauces, soups and teas. It is a medicinal plant too. Around the world, the gentle healing properties of rose make a valuable addition to the natural apothecary cabinet.

Britain's native wild roses have been open to discussion by botanists for years because of the wide variations between different species and hybrids. However, most agree on five distinct species: Dog Rose (*R. canina*), field rose (*R. arvensis*), sweet briar (*R. rubiginosa*), burnet rose (*R. spinosissima*), and downy rose (*R. villosa*).

The Dog Rose, a scrambling, prickly climber with delicate, whitish-pink flowers, is the topic of this chapter, but other species will often take centre stage. Like all wild roses, the Dog Rose must constantly compete with its cultivated cousins for recognition.

Its subtle-scented flowers appear in early summer in shades of white to pink. Gabrielle Hatfield says Dog Rose is one of the longest living plants: "A bush growing in Hildesheim in Germany was said to have been planted there in AD 850 by Emperor Charlemagne's son". So we don't forget the beauty of a wild rose forever in the shadow of its garden relatives, she writes:

> Viewed from a distance, a flowering English rosebush looks as though a flock of pink butterflies has perched on it ... you see a jewel-like beauty, with a golden crown of stamens protected by delicate petals.

The deep orangey-red fruit – the rosehip – is traditionally the most-used part of the plant. Mrs Grieve wrote in her A Modern Herbal:

Rosehips were long official in the British Pharmacopoeia for refrigerant and astringent properties but are now discarded and only used in medicine to prepare the confection of hips used in conjunction with other drugs.

The Dog Rose was named for the belief that it cured the bite of rabid dogs. Roman physician Pliny the Elder in the 1st century told the story of a woman who received a message in a dream. The woman was asked to send her son, a soldier, a decoction of wild (dog) rose root. The decoction, known to the Greeks as Cynorrhodon, cured a mad dog's bite.

Other sources imply that dog is a corruption of dagger referring to the plant's jagged-edged leaves. It has been suggested the dog in Dog Rose was meant in a derogatory sense, implying that Dog Rose was of little worth in the garden. Both alternatives contradict the Greek story of the flower's origins. Rest assured, Dog Rose is worthy of a place in our history and culture. Remains of its fruits are dated back to prehistoric settlements and prove their value to early societies.

FOOD

The edible orange pulp of the rose fruit (or rosehip) was once collected in Europe when few other fruits were available. Ancient Greek physician Galen in the 3rd century remarked that country people gathered them.

Gerard wrote (probably about Dog Rose): "The fruit when it is ripe maketh the most pleasante meats and banketting dishes as tartes and such-like". Another early text says: "Children with great delight eat the berries thereof when they are ripe and make chains and other pretty geegaws of the fruit; cookes and gentlewomen make tarts and such-like dishes for pleasure."

The rosehips of all roses are edible, but they can vary in flavour – some are bitter, and others taste like raspberries.

Rosehips can be a wonderful winter treat if you know how to eat them. Francois Couplan gives this advice:

They become soft with the frosts and generally acquire a pleasant sweet, acid and aromatic taste. They can be eaten as such, pressing the hips delicately between the fingers in order to let the pulp out at the base, like a natural jam out of a tube.

After the fruits dry on the bushes in late winter and early spring, the rosehips can be ground into powder to mix with flour and make bread, cakes, cookies and porridge. However, despite their reputation as a fruit, this is deceiving. The actual fruit is the hairy seeds inside the fleshy orange-red berry.

In the Second World War of the 20th century, the British government utilised rosehips as a good source of vitamin C in the absence of citrus fruits for rations.

> In 1941 the Ministry of Health put forward a scheme for collection of rosehips, which had been found to contain twenty times the amount of vitamin C in oranges, and in that year 120 tons were gathered by voluntary collectors. The next year the scheme was transferred to the Vegetable Drugs Committee of the Ministry of Supply and 344 tons were gathered. By 1943 the redoubtable County Herb Committees were brought in to organise the collection, and for the next three years the harvest averaged 450 tons. The resulting syrup was sold through ordinary retailers at a controlled price of 9d a six-ounce (170 ml) bottle. Mothers and children were able to obtain it in larger quantities, and at reduced prices, from Welfare Clinics.
>
> — RICHARD MABEY

The collection of rosehips up-and-down the country was a community effort by schools, voluntary groups and the Women's Institute. This wartime project resulted in the collection of 2,000 tons of rosehips by the end of the war.

> The collection was just one of the many things organised by my school - Gaynes, Upminster - and was one of many things we were expected to do for the war effort from writing ration books to collecting razor blades! We were definitely not paid for any war effort activities.
>
> — ROY VICKERY

Shopkeepers sold rosehip syrup throughout the 60s and the 70s, but today it is only available from specialist suppliers and usually made from fruits imported from Chile.

Wild roses flourish in Britain and Ireland with around twelve native species and many more hybrids. They are widespread in different habitats, from hedgerows and waste grounds to dunes and heaths. As one of the most popular garden plants, roses feature in plant lore and are often used for cut flowers.

The similarities in appearance make it tricky to identify which species is which, and numerous hybrids are making specific identification difficult.

That being said, all the wild roses are edible. The most popular native ones are:

Rosa agrestis (Small-leaved sweet-briar), *Rosa arvensis* (Field or trailing Rose), *Rosa caesia subsp. caesia* (Hairy dog-rose), *Rosa caesia subsp. glaucac* (Glaucous dog-rose), *Rosa canina* (Dog Rose), *Rosa micrantha* (Small-flowered Sweet-briar), *Rosa mollis* (Soft downy rose), *Rosa obtusifolia* (Round-leaved dog-rose), *Rosa pimpinellifolia* (Burnet rose), *Rosa rubiginosa* (Sweet briar), *Rosa sherardii* (Sherard's downy rose), *Rosa stylosa* (Short-styled field rose), *Rosa tomentosa* (Harsh downy-rose).

As well as a common non-native called *Rosa rugosa* (Japanese rose). Originating in China but found all over the country, especially in cities. All species have similar uses and produce rosehips.

The link between the fruit and vitamin C was probably not made in ancient times, but we can be pretty confident that those wild rosehips were gathered as food. The fruit made jams, jellies, pies, stews, tea and wine; the petals and leaves were brewed for tea. The berries are best collected after frost, which improves their flavour.

Failing a frosty Autumn/Winter, you can always pop them in a freezer until they are just beginning to freeze, then remove and allow them to come to room temperature before using. Don't let them become frozen solid.

The freezing process mimics frost and breaks the cell walls down, enabling more liquid and flavour to come out.

Rosehips were known as Johnnie Magories or Johnny Magoreys in eastern Ireland, although some sources suggest the nickname was confused with Hawthorn fruits.

Peter Wyse Jackson mentions a rhyme associated with the name:

> *I'll tell you a story of Johnnie Magory;*
> *He went to the wood and shot a Tory.*

In Britain and Ireland, children picked rosehips to play a prank on each other. The hairy seeds were put down the victim's neck and caused terrible itching. This game led to the common names' itchy-backs', 'itchy-berries' and 'itchypoos' for the rose fruits.

A school prank in east Hertfordshire, 1945–50 ... the most awful itching material was made from rose hips - the hairs on the seeds being put down someone's neck - a bath and complete change of clothing being the only cure.

— ROY VICKERY

Few specific uses of Dog Rose in Irish folk medicine are recorded by Jackson save for a nod towards its use to castrate animals. He writes that briar roses, which may refer to Dog Rose, were collected for their shoots to make baskets.

In her A Modern Herbal, Mrs Grieve helpfully referred to the specific uses of different species under her entry on Wild Roses:

> The leaves of Dog Rose made a pleasantly scented tea with a light astringent taste. The fragrance of the flowers is so subtle that they are not much good for distillation into scented oils and perfumes.

The Dog Rose's close relative sweet briar (*R. rubiginosa*) has sweet-scented leaves (again, the flowers are almost without scent), but it is not collected today for its essence. Grieve notes a common mistake – that briarwood pipes were made from sweet briar; they were in fact made from an entirely unrelated plant, the tree heath (*Erica arborea*). She wrote relatively little about the field rose or downy rose other than the former is an ornament of the hedgerows.

The fruit of the Burnet Rose (*R. pimpinellifolia*) was once used to dye silk and muslin and produces a delicious peach colour.

The delicate aroma of wild roses can enhance such a variety of dishes that their usefulness in the kitchen is almost unending.

The prolific garden writer and broadcaster Frances Perry, who died in 1993, lists ten uses for rose petals: "rose wine, rose in brandy, rose vinegar, rhubarb and rose-petal jam, rose honey, rose and coconut candies, Turkish delight, rose drops, crystallised rose petals, and rose-petal jelly".

The rosehips of Dog Rose are a valuable fruit for jams, jellies, syrups, soups, teas, wine and liqueurs. And Dog Rose flowers can be eaten in salads or candied or preserved for vinegar, honey and brandy.

To add a touch of Dog Rose to any recipe you only need a little imagination: drop a couple of petals into homemade lemonade, stir the flowers and fruits into conserves, pies and tart fillings or sugar-frost the petals for ice cream.

The delights of rose tea and jellies are not constrained to a handful of species. Turkey is the capital of the rose and home to about 25% of all rose species from coastal regions to mountain ranges.

In Anatolia, which has the largest population of native roses, the fruits of roses (rosehips) have been gathered as food for centuries. Famous roses like *R. gallica* and *R. damascena* have been commercially harvested for the highly prized attar of roses and rose water.

The rose is the star of Turkey's flora used for many medicinal, culinary and domestic purposes. In addition, jams, marmalades, syrups, a fruit paste called marmelat, and teas are enjoyed for both their flavour and purported health-giving benefits.

A Turkish recipe for rose-petal jam is popular in the Middle East – it's reportedly very sweet and eaten with yoghurt.

In China, rose petals are added as flavouring to black tea. In other parts of the Middle East, certain species are collected for their petals and made into jam.

The rose oil distilled in southern France and Bulgary uses two Asian species: *R. alba* and *R. damascena*. It is one of the most expensive essential oils, as one ton of fresh petals yields only one-half pint of oil.

The byproduct of this distillation process is rosewater, which is widely used in the eastern Mediterranean for making confectionary treats mixed with honey and almonds. It is also used by the food industry as flavouring and by the cosmetic industry as a fragrance and beautifying ingredient in soaps, eyewashes, cleansers and lotions.

In the Americas, the fruits and flowers of *R. blanda*, the state flower of North Dakota, are enjoyed as a wild edible. Likewise, *R. californica* yields edible fruits, called macuatas in Spanish, eaten raw or steamed.

North America's native rose species, *R. caroline*, has edible petals, stems, leaves, fruit, and roots. The petals make a pretty addition to salads or as a garnish or can be infused into ice cubes or ice lollies. The leaves can be used as a raw salad leaf; you can slice even the bulbous parts for salads. The fruits make jam, jellies and sweets. Finally, the stem, root and all other parts can be brewed to make tea.

The fruits of various rose species were collected in Canada by native tribes. The prickly rose (*R. acicularis*) was most commonly eaten. It was gathered from late summer to winter when the flavour of the hips was improved by frost.

It was a valuable food source when few other berries grew in winter, but the seeds sometimes caused itchy bottom due to tiny hairs that irritated the digestive tract. Fisherman Lake Slave people picked the fruits to avoid starvation and boiled them as a tea or brew. The fresh flower petals were eaten in summer or made into tea.

In Alaska, rosehips were a taste of the wild for the Inupiaq Inuits. The rinds were mashed with seal oil and water, sweetened to make a pudding, or eaten with chewed, dried salmon tails. The fruits were frozen or dried, but today are made into syrup, jam, jelly and marmalade. The Tanaina tribe mix rosehips with grease or fish eggs or whip them with fat to make ice cream.

Rosehips are an emergency food for bears as well as people. They gorge on the fruits before winter hibernation.

How to Dry and Store Rosehips

Pick as many rose hips as you think you need to last you until next year. I also wash them first. After washing your rose hips, dry them in the sun on newspaper. Then top and tail them by removing the stalk and the little pointy bit where the flower was. This isn't important, but I do it. Dry them whole. For convenience, use a food dehydrator. Dehydration takes about 5-6 hours. But this is "wild stuff", so times may vary depending on the quality of the hips, how many you're drying etc.

Next, put them in a food processor and process until the hips and seeds are broken into small pieces, but not so small that you have turned them into dust. Tip the contents into a metal sieve, and just shake to remove all those pesky hairs that can irritate some people. Discard the hairs. Pour the dried rose hips into a jar or airtight container, and consume at will. There is no need to go to the trouble of removing the seeds.

Rose Petal Honey

- 1 clean jar with screw top lid.
- 1 jar of light, clear honey.
- A tub of Rosa rugosa petals.

Finely chop the rose petals, then put them into your empty jar and pour over the honey. Stir well, then allow to sit on a windowsill in sunlight. The petals will all rise to the top, so add more carefully, stirring them. You might think you have filled the jar up, but keep adding more until the honey, and rose petal mixture is nearly overflowing. Cap and return to the windowsill. Add more petals if there is honey showing as the petals try and separate. It's all a guesstimate with this recipe. Leave for a couple of weeks and then use on hot buttered toasted tea cakes or just plain toast. Stir into porridge.

Rosehip Soup With Roasted Chilli & Smoked Tofu

- 600g Japanese rosehips (Rosa rugosa)
- 3 red chillies
- 200g smoked tofu
- 2 Echalion shallots (sliced)
- 2 garlic cloves (chopped)
- 500ml chicken stock
- 500ml rosehip juice

Cover rosehips with water and simmer for 20 minutes. Using a potato masher, mash the hips halfway through the simmering time. Strain the rosehip mixture through a muslin or jelly bag overnight to remove hairs and seeds. Roast the chillies until just turning brown but not burnt. Put into a plastic bag or Tupperware and allow to sweat. This makes removing the skins easier. Then skin them and roughly chop. In a saucepan, fry the shallots until translucent, then combine the rosehip liquid, chicken stock, roasted chillies, and diced smoked tofu. Simmer for 10 minutes, then blend to desired consistency.

Rosehip Syrup

- 1kg rosehips
- 3 litres of water
- 500g dark brown soft sugar

Bring to boil 2 litres of water. Chop rosehips in a food processor until mashed up, then add to boiling water. Bring water back to a boil, then remove from heat and allow to steep for 20 minutes. Pour rosehips and liquid into a scalded jelly bag and let the juice to drip overnight. Gently squeeze the jelly bag to extract as much liquid as possible. Be careful not to rip the bag.

Add rosehip pulp back to a saucepan containing 1 litre of water and bring back to the boil. Then remove from heat and allow the contents to steep for another 20 minutes before straining through the jelly bag. Add sugar to the strained rosehip liquid and dissolve, simmer for five minutes, then pour into hot, sterilised bottles. Makes: Approximately 2 litres.

MEDICINE

In an ancient system of medicine, four humours illustrated the workings of the human body. These humours had different qualities or temperaments, and an imbalance of one of these qualities could cause disease.

Writing under this system in the 12th century, German abbess Hildegard von Bingen said the rose (referring to the group Rosa in general) was cold and that "this same coldness has a useful temperament in it".

Its corresponding virtues were drawing and strengthening. Thus the rose would draw out impurities and boost the healing power of other medicines.

But let whoever has a weeping ulcer on his or her body, place a rose leaf over it and draw out the pus. But rose also strengthens any potion or ointment or any other medication when it is added to it.

In the Doctrine of Signatures, which assigned healing properties to plants that resembled parts of the body, Dog Rose was indicated for facial redness. A cloth was sOaked in the flower water and applied to the hot face to allow its cooling nature to take effect. Still, today rose water (not necessarily that made from the petals of Dog Rose) is marketed as a refreshing, cooling tonic for the skin.

In Ireland, Dog Rose didn't have a particular use in herbal medicine. Coitir writes: "It was traditionally lumped in with bramble under the common name of 'brier', it is possible that some of the herbal remedies for that plant in fact involve dog-rose." The wild species known as sweet briar (*R. rubiginosa*) was used in Country Longford as a decoction to cure jaundice.

The roses grown in gardens, particularly red roses, were preferred over wild varieties in traditional herbal medicine. For example, English herbalist John Pechey (1655-1716) wrote that the "red rose is astringent and bitter: It comforts the Heart and strengthens the Stomach"; he goes on to prescribe the herb for headaches, fluxes (perhaps referring to blood in the urine or stools) and coughs.

In the 18th century, healers recommended red roses to prevent abortion when taken as a conserve. In the 19th century, an infusion of red roses was recommended as an astringent gargle for a sore mouth. An entry in the British Pharmacopoeia in 1914 for red rose petals refers to *R. gallica*. A native rose of North America, *R.*

caroline, has been used in herbal medicine to clear sinuses and treat boils, sores and wounds.

A surprising addition to early medical texts is the rose gall made by the larvae of the gall wasp on Dog Roses and on some other species, which was sold in Britain by apothecaries. These blights upon the rose were valued as a healing remedy for various disorders. Also known as Briar Balls or Robin Redbreast's Cushions, healers took the powdered galls for stones in the body, colic, and a diuretic (to increase urination). A gipsy remedy was to boil the gall with black sugar to treat whooping cough. As a healing amulet, galls could be hung at home to ward off rheumatism or piles, placed under the pillow to relieve the cramp, or carried in the pocket to prevent toothache.

In the 16th century, English herbalist John Gerard (1545–1612) quoted Pliny, who suggested galls mixed with honey and ashes cured hair loss. In the Middle Ages, rose galls, known as Bedeguar, induced sleep if placed under the pillow. Vickery writes they were worn by schoolboys "as a charm to prevent a flogging".

Grigson suggests that these galls were more valuable to folk medicine than the wild rose itself:

> Garden roses were used against a hundred ills, from St Anthony's Fire to the French pox; but medicine had recourse to the wild rose for one thing – the reddish-yellow bedeguar or Robin's pincushion, the gall made by the gall wasp *Rhodites rosae*.

The fruit of the rose was the plant in which vitamin C was first discovered. In addition, rosehips were used as a preventative for colds and ailments like inflamed or bleeding gums. Traditionally, the fruit has been used to treat kidney and gall stones and is a diuretic and laxative.

As a medicinal herb today, the rosehips of Dog Rose are indicated for a wide range of conditions from headaches, sore throats, infections, sciatica, gout, rheumatism, stress and nervousness. The fruit's antioxidant compounds and tannins are thought to be responsible for their popularity in treating stress and infection.

The Dog Rose has been used by herbalists specifically for those times when you need a gentle remedy for diarrhoea. The syrup is gentle enough to be given to babies as a nutritional supplement. It is even listed as a treatment for certain types of cancer. Still, it's crucial to ask your doctor before taking any herbal supplement for cancer or other serious medical condition.

If you want to drink tea for beautiful skin, rosehip infusions are said to be rich in collagen, as well as vitamin C, which helps to plump up cells and, as a bonus, boost immunity to viral infections. In addition, vitamin C is valued in cosmetics for its ability to strengthen capillary fragility and connective tissues.

In 2007 Ercisli looked at the chemistry of rose fruits. Out of the six fruits included in the study, *R. canina* had the highest level of antioxidants. In addition, the fruit's high vitamin C content has made it a popular cold remedy in Turkey for generations.

The research revealed that all native species of rose fruits in Turkey are rich sources of carbohydrates, vitamin C, antioxidants, and other minerals. Therefore, an understanding of the variations between species was vital for plant breeding in the future.

Barros and team (2010) examined the nutritional value of rose fruits, strawberry-tree berries and sloes. All the wild fruits proved valuable sources of antioxidants, with the highest antioxidant activity found in rose fruits.

The study was based upon the traditional uses for wild fruits in Portugal. Focusing on rosehips, several different species have been identified. The fruit of a group of scrambling roses, indigenous to Europe, northwest Africa and western Asia, are collected to treat colds, flu, minor infections, diarrhoea, and as an anti-inflammatory for muscular and joint problems.

In the Trás-os-Montes region, the fruit of *R. canina* and *R. corymbifera* are interchangeably used in folk medicine. In addition, local children were given raw rosehips as snacks in late summer.

In north-eastern Portugal, people preserved the fruits over winter for use in jams, marmalades, spirits and infusions widely consumed for their preventative or curative properties.

Overall, the wild fruits were shown to be useful for satisfying hunger because of their carbohydrate content; other nutrients such as fats, fibre and water content varied depending on growing conditions. In addition, the rose fruits had the highest content of essential fatty acids, which can help reduce cholesterol.

The study illustrated the abundant levels of vitamin C in rosehips along with the highest antioxidant activity out of the three fruits. This could contribute to understanding their role in folk medicine for chronic diseases caused by oxidative stress in the body.

Based on their antioxidant value, a 2011 study by Barros and team explored the potential commercial uses for *R. canina* fruits, such as preventing fats from turning rancid in foods or as a supplement to reduce the effects of ageing.

Egea and team (2010) examined the potential antioxidant activity in six edible wild fruits, including *R. canina*. The study found that antioxidant activity was highest in rose fruits, which suggested the possible use of *R. canina* as a natural antioxidant to replace nutritional supplements.

The authors based their study on the social, cultural and economic value of wild edibles in the Mediterranean diet. Their aim to confirm the nutritional advantage of these types of food and their importance to human health:

> The consumption of fruits with a high antioxidant composition has been associated with a lowered incidence of degenerative diseases, including cancer, heart disease, inflammation, arthritis, immune system decline, brain dysfunction, and cataracts.

Referring to *R. canina*, the authors stated it must be "highlighted for showing a much higher antioxidant activity and phytonutrient concentration (phenolic and carotenoid) than the rest of the fruits."

Kirkeskov and team (2011) studied the effects of *R. canina* on rheumatoid arthritis. They found that a powder made from the plant and given to patients for one month did not affect their symptoms.

An online analysis of the wild rosehips of the northern plains Indians reveals exceptional nutritional values per 100 g serving. Based on recommended daily allowances of vitamins and minerals, the fruits provide 710% vitamin C, 87% vitamin A, 17% calcium and 6% iron, a good source of vitamins E and K, and minerals such as magnesium, manganese, and potassium.

Özcan (2002) evaluated the nutritional content of *R. canina* seed and oils. He concluded that rose oils are rich in essential fatty acids. The seeds are also a valuable source of oils and minerals; the quality of fatty acids depended on the variety of rose fruits and the growing conditions.

SAFETY NOTE

Tiny hairs on fresh or dried rosehips might irritate the mouth and throat. This might be a concern if eating raw fruits because commercial processing removes the hairs.

The plant is generally well-tolerated as a medicinal herb or food with few reports of allergic reactions.

Dog Rose's safety during pregnancy or when breastfeeding is unknown.

GUELDER ROSE
Viburnum opulus

FAMILY

Viburnaceae.

BOTANICAL DESCRIPTION

Height: grows as a small shrub or tree up to 5 m (16.5 ft). Leaves: growing on a tender leafstalk, the leaves are divided into three or five broad angular lobes, which can be toothed; in August, the leaves turn rich purple before they fall. Flowers: fertile flowers are pinkish-white in bud, producing red, glossy drupes; large plate-like, outer, white flowers are sterile. Stems: slender leafstalks.

FLOWERS

May to July.

STATUS

Perennial. Native.

HABITAT

Deciduous woodland, hedgerows, scrub.

OVERVIEW

> *Along wet ditches, the flowers toss and sparkle in a May wind.*

Geoffrey Grigson tells us that the name Guelder Rose properly belongs to the variety roseum, a familiar garden bush that is "planted so often near the front door of farmhouses and cottages, and splendid with its snowballs of blossom in May". It is not related to the rose family. The garden variety may have been cultivated at Guelders, on the frontier between Germany and Holland, as the rhyme below suggests:

> *Sambucus too from Gueldria's Plains will come,*
> *Drest in white Robes she shows a Roselike bloom,*
> *Be kind, and give the lovely Stranger Room.*

On the other hand, Angela Paine writes that the true Guelder Rose should not be confused with the garden variety: "which Bentham and Hooker describe as a monstrosity, since all the flowers are enlarged and barren, giving the flower heads a globular shape like snowballs".

The English botanist and herbalist John Gerard (1545–1612) knew the plant as rose elder or gelders rose. He wrote that it's "goodly flowers of a white colour, spinckled or dashed heere and there with a light and thinne carnation colour".

In his Herbal (1597), Gerard described the plant as:

> The Rose Elder is called in Latine Sambucus Rosea and Sambucus aquatic…In English Gelders Rose and Rose Elder". English poet Geoffrey Chaucer (1343–1400) wrote about Guelder Rose berries, or 'gaitre-berries', and advised: "pick them right as they grow and ete hem in.

Guelder Rose (*Viburnum opulus*), is also known as crampbark or crampbush.

FOOD

In northern Europe, such as in Norway and Sweden, the Guelder Rose is used to flavour a paste of honey and flour.

In Estonia, the fruits have been eaten as a snack and used in baking bread, added to porridge, soup and pies, made into jams, syrups, desserts or juices, and used as an additive in vodka. Cooks used Guelder Rose fruits to fill scraping cakes (kaapekakk), traditional rye bread dough. In Poland, this wild edible has is used for making wine, syrup and jams.

In Russia, the fruits were eaten fresh after freezing and again used in porridge, for baking, making jams, jellies and marmalade, pastes, vinegar, mousse, pie fillings, as a condiment to meat. The fruits were also used as a substitute for tea or roasted as a substitute for coffee. However, the traditional food use of berries, such as guelder, has declined in Russia, write Shikov and team (2017), because of the bitter, astringent taste of the berries.

However, in the mid 19th century, Guelder Rose fruits were popular in Tver province of Russia as an ingredient for kulaga, a malt flour-based porridge. The fruits were prepared with flour and honey for "urban residents, not excluding the nobility". In Pskov province, residents were nicknamed kalinniki, because of their traditional porridge cooked with Guelder Rose. In Siberia, the fruits of Guelder Rose were fermented with flour and distilled to produce a spirit.

John F Richards writes that Russian forests do not offer the same variety of edible nuts as found in the forests of western Europe. Still, they do offer a variety of berries, including Guelder Rose.

> Every peasant family picked hundreds of kilograms of barberries (Berberis vulgaris), cowberries (Vaccinium vitis idaea), bogberries

(Vaccinium oxycoccus)…They picked hips of the Dog Rose (Rosa canina) and cinnamon rose (Rosa cinnamomea), the fruits of the Guelder Rose (Viburnum opulus)…Whether eaten fresh, combined with honey in preserves or added to kvass as a flavoring element, berries in quantities such as these contributed significant amounts of vitamins and calories to the peasant diet.

A Guelder Rose by any other name. Here is where some confusion lies. In Canada and North America, Guelder Rose is often known as the European cranberry bush. However, *Viburnum opulus* is not related to the true cranberry.

Merritt Lyndon Fernald and Alfred Charles Kinsey write that highbush cranberries are generally known in northern American states and Canada. In those regions where bog-cranberries are not well known, they are often served as cranberries.

Canadians use the Guelder Rose fruits as a substitute for cranberries and to make jelly, although only the cooked fruits are eaten as the raw fruit is not safe to eat. Guelder Rose jelly is delicious as an accompaniment to roasted meat. In addition, these sour, bright red fruits are made into preserves, sauces and wine; apparently, a yellow-fruited cultivar can also be used for wine.

Pick the berries in autumn after they have been softened and sweetened by freezing, although, in this era of climate change, it is advisable to freeze, then defrost them.

The berries have a good flavour. However, some have compared the fragrance to dirty socks. You can alleviate it for those who don't appreciate the odour by adding lemon or orange peel to the mix. Due to being frozen, the berries used to make jams, jellies, and preserves require the addition of pectin. Early settlers to the Americas, however, discovered that berries not fully ripened did not require pectin. Therefore, I use Crab Apple, which is high in pectin.

Native American Indians added these bush cranberries to bear grease or, early in the year, mixed them with Saskatoon Serviceberry (*Amelanchier alnifolia*). Sometimes the boiled fruits were mixed in oil and whipped with fresh snow to make a frothy dessert. The fruits make excellent winter survival food as they remain on the branches all winter. In addition, the berries can be steeped in hot water to make tea or juiced for cold drinks.

Arthur Haines says that *V. opulus* is called Ipiminaks by the Passamaquoddy people. The fruit is called Ipimin, meaning leaf berry. The fruits were eaten by the Chippewa, Iroquois, Maliseet, Menominee, Okanagan, Quebec, Algonquin, and Thompson.

Guelder Rose Jelly

- 800g Guelder Rose fruits (make sure you pick them soft)
- 2 peeled oranges (chopped)
- 12 Crab Apples (chopped)
- 500ml of cold water
- sugar

Put the Guelder Rose fruits, oranges, Crab Apples and water into a heavy-bottomed pan and bring to a simmer. Simmer for 15 minutes, using a potato masher to mash the mixture occasionally. Strain overnight or for 12 hours by pouring the mixture through a muslin cloth or jelly bag. Do not squeeze the pulp as this will result in a cloudy jelly.

Next, measure out the liquid, and for every 500ml, add 500g of white or brown sugar. Heat the sugar mixture stirring continuously until the sugar has melted, and allow it to come to a gentle simmer. Simmer for between 15-20 minutes or until the liquid has reached the setting point.

The setting point is when you can put a little bit of the juice on a plate and allow it to cool somewhat, then push your finger through the juice. If it doesn't automatically fall back into itself and stays at the point you pushed it to; then it's ready. Important: Make sure you don't over simmer the juice as you might end up with toffee.

Wash your jars and lids with hot soapy water, sterilise them by placing wet into a 120C oven until they are dry. Take out of the oven, cool for about 5 minutes, then pour the hot Guelder Rose liquid into the jars. Allow to cool down, then screw on the lids.

Kaluga

- 250g Guelder Rose fruit
- 1tbsp butter
- 4 tbsp of rye flour
- 2-3 tbsp of honey
- 500ml of water
- 1 tbsp of sugar

Place the Guelder Rose fruit in a saucepan and add 500ml of water. Bring to the boil and simmer for 10 minutes. Take the saucepan off the heat. In a bowl, mix the butter, flour, sugar and honey and combine well. Add to the saucepan and stir in or use a whisk. It would be best if you avoided lumps. Easier said than done. Then return the saucepan to heat, and stir until it starts to thicken. It should be the consistency of thick cream. Serve like porridge.

MEDICINE

Gerard wrote that an infusion of the bark of Guelder Rose was used to treat cramp, which is why the plant was also known as crampbark, or crampbush.

In Europe, Guelder Rose was primarily used as Polish or Romanian folk medicine. Today, the herb is still recognised as a medicinal plant in Poland, Romania and Russia. In Russia, for example, a brandy called Nastoika is made from berries and taken for peptic ulcers. The Russians would also make a medicinal decoction from the bark. In Poland, Guelder Rose is made into cough syrup.

By the 19th century, however, the herb achieved more popularity as a medicinal plant in North America than it did in northern and western Europe.

Native American Indians know the plant as crampbark or highbush cranberry bark and used the bark as a diuretic and sedative. The Meskwaki people took crampbark for cramps and pains, and the Penobscot and Micmac tribes used the berries to treat glandular problems such as mumps and swellings. The Iroquois used the plant for liver diseases and blood disorders, and the Montagnais Indians made a decoction for sore eyes.

In North Carolina, Tennessee and Kentucky, the bark is used in local folk medicine for its antispasmodic effects and as a sedative.

In Japan, guelder fruit is prepared as vinegar to treat cirrhosis of the liver.

In India, the native North American variety called cranberry bush (*V. opulus var. americanum*) is imported for use in Indian herbal medicine. The bark is used as a diuretic and uterine tonic.

Women have used Guelder Rose bark for hundreds of years to help with menstrual cramps. It has been used to treat very painful menstrual flows (such as dysmenorrhoea), endometriosis (a painful condition when pieces of the endometrium grow outside the uterus in the pelvis or abdominal wall), or fibroids. Paine tells us:

In 1966 Jarboe and his co-workers tested an extract of Guelder Rose bark on uterine muscle, and they found that it had a relaxing effect; and in 1972 Nicholson isolated viopudial, the compound responsible for this.

As a herbal remedy, crampbark has been used for high blood pressure and circulatory complaints.

The bark can also relieve hiccups, pain, and spasms in muscles, stomach, and intestines. Mrs Grieve writes that the plant has also been used in herbal medicine for spasms, fits, convulsions, lockjaw, palpitations, heart disease, and rheumatism. In addition, some herbalists recommend Guelder Rose to bring relief to stiff joints and muscles caused by arthritis:

> As the muscles relax, blood flow to the area improves, waste products such as lactic acid are removed and normal function can return.

The plant has been recommended for earache, acute bronchitis, and bedwetting in children. In addition, it may be used for colic and irritable bowel syndrome, and Guelder Rose mixed with lobelia is a remedy for night cramps and back pain.

Haines supports these uses for the plant due to the polyphenols contained in *V. opulus*, "including the coumarins scopoletin and scopoline, the hydroquinones arbutin and methyl arbutin, and catechins (kinds of tannins)". These chemical constituents give the plant antispasmodic, anti-inflammatory, astringent, emmenagogue, hypotensive, and nervine actions.

Sagdic and team (2006) investigated cranberry fruit extract's antibacterial and antioxidant actions (*V. opulus*), or Gilaburu, as the plant is known in Turkey. Although they found the antioxidant activity significant, antibacterial actions were also impressive, with bacterial growth inhibited at 10% and 15% concentrations of cranberry fruit extract.

Rop and team (2010) write that *V. opulus* is a "promising crop plant in human nutrition" due to its high polyphenolic content and antioxidant activity".

The US Pharmacopeia once included the plant. It has been introduced into the UK's National Formulary as a fluid extract and compound tincture for use as a nerve sedative and antispasmodic in asthma and hysteria. Its chemistry is identical to the species more widely used in the US – Blackhaw (*Viburnum prunifolium*).

SAFETY NOTE

Jackson suggests that Guelder Rose is considered toxic in some countries and advises using the plant sparingly. Symptoms of poisoning may include gastrointestinal upset, vomiting, diarrhoea, and collapsing; some reports suggest the poisoning may potentially be fatal.

Duke notes that the herb should not be used by anyone with kidney stones and that large overdoses may cause "coma, dry mouth, dyspnea, irregular movements, nausea, and irregular speech". In Canada, regulations state that crampbark cannot be used as a non-medicinal ingredient for oral-use products.

Kershaw echoes these cautionary notes and writes that the bark tea has caused nausea and vomiting, whereas Quattrocchi suggests those who eat the berries may have mild symptoms. Severe cases of poisoning by crampbark berries were reported in 19th-century literature, according to Mills and Bone; no official claims of poisoning by the berries have been recorded in Britain.

Mills and Bone write that there are no harmful effects from the use of crampbark in pregnancy, while other texts suggest you should not use it during pregnancy. In any case, always check with your doctor or midwife before taking any herbal remedy during pregnancy. Mild cases of poisoning in children have been reported as a result of overeating the berries.

HAWTHORN
Crataegus monogyna

FAMILY

Rosaceae.

BOTANICAL DESCRIPTION

Height: a small deciduous tree or shrub growing up to 6 m tall. Flowers: small, white, sometimes pink, blossoms forming clusters. Leaves: fan-shaped, ovate, bright, green leaves with toothed margins. Root and stem: long, hard woody roots protruding a stem with spiny branches. Foliage: thorny, twisting branches.

FLOWERS

April to June.

STATUS

Perennial. Native.

HABITAT

Deciduous woodland, hedgerows, scrub.

OVERVIEW

Hawthorn (*Crataegus monogyna*) is a distinctive-looking tree or shrub with impenetrable thorny branches and strongly scented white blossoms. These recognisable characteristics have made it both much-loved and much-feared in plant lore.

Its origin as a lightning tree in myth and legend associates Hawthorn with magical qualities and various superstitions. Still, above all, it is a tree of new life, love and new beginnings. The Hawthorn's May blossom marks the end of spring and the beginning of summer.

In Ireland, Hawthorn is one of the most familiar and most significant trees in Ireland – it is sometimes called the May Bush in Ireland. However, it shares many common magical attributes and plant lore with other trees in Ireland, Britain and Europe.

In herbal medicine, Hawthorn is 'the father of the heart' because the flowers, fruits and leaves contain antioxidant compounds that have been used to treat various heart conditions.

FOOD

Hawthorn berries, or haws, were a source of food in ancient Ireland. The seeds have been found in excavations of Viking Dublin dating back more than 1,000 years. Hawthorn trees are often heavy with berries in late autumn when other native fruits have faded. There was an old Irish saying: 'When all fruit fails, then welcome haw'. An advantage of picking the berries later in the season is that they become somewhat tastier and sweeter.

More superstitious folk claimed that the berries were best eaten after Halloween when the witches had flown over them. However, it is more likely that the first frosts improved the berries' flavour, ready for making hedgerow jams and country wines. In some parts of Britain, the fruits are called pixie pears, cuckoo's beads and chucky cheese.

Hawthorn berries (haws) have a distinctive, perhaps acquired, taste. They are mildly sweet but not particularly juicy. Haws can be picked to make jam, jellies, marmalades, wine. Hawthorn jelly can be used as an alternative to red currant jelly to serve with meat dishes. In Scotland, Hawthorn berries have been used, to a limited extent, in commercial jam mixes.

The berries were picked and eaten in other countries, such as Portugal, Spain, Italy, Slovenia, Bosnia-Herzegovina, Cyprus, Turkey, Tunisia and Morocco, either as snacks or added to traditional dishes, such as desserts, or even stored for winter. However, some trees bear bigger, juicier fruits, so haws were sometimes preferred as a children's snack or reserved for times of scarcity as a famine food.

During World War I, the young leaves were used as a tea and tobacco substitute, and the seeds were ground as a coffee substitute. During World War II, the fruit was finely ground as an ingredient to make bread. This usage was also recorded in Ireland as a poor man's flour – the ground dried fruit sold in markets could be reduced to meal and eaten as a bread substitute.

Throughout Europe, Hawthorn berries have at certain times been used as a flour additive for making bread and cakes. In parts of Africa, Hawthorn berries were also ground and added to flour. However, the berries were only used as a source of food by African tribesmen up until the 19th century, when they again became a folk medicine.

In Canada, haws were eaten fresh or dried (in the absence of other berries) by various tribespeople, including the Haida, Coast Tsimshian, Nuu-chah-nulth, Kwakwaka'wakw, Nuxalk (Bella Coola), Straits, Halkomelem, Okanagan-Colville, Lillooet, Shuswap, Kootenay, Gitksan, Nishga and Blackfoot. The haws' dryness was counteracted by mixing with oily foods, such as salmon roe, marmot fat, or bear fat. The Okanagan-Colville and Lillooet mashed and dried haws into thin cakes to dip in soup or boil with deer fat and bone marrow.

Hawthorn makes an excellent country wine. The flower wine has a fresh, floral taste, and the fruit wine is richer and full-bodied. Hawthorn wine has been enjoyed in many countries, from rural Britain to parts of Russia and China. In Spain, Italy and Slovenia, the fruits were macerated in liquor or brandy, sometimes with other herbs, to make a liqueur.

For berry connoisseurs, the juiciness of the berries may depend on the variety of Hawthorn. Fernald and Kinsey write:

> The planted English Hawthorn has an inferior fruit, and the superior quality of some of the native American Haws was early recognised by Europeans. The jelly from the better species of Haw requires comparatively little sugar.

Berries of the English species when ripe taste like a avocado and make a tolerable jelly if simmered for a long time with Crab Apples to bring out the juices and to provide more pectin. The sourness of the berries is considered good for digestion.

The white flowers are edible, despite their unusual smell, and have a variety of uses, including to flavour puddings or to add to fruit salads, or other desserts, as decoration. You can also use them to make wine or liqueur when mixed with sugar and brandy.

Foragers should not ignore the buds and young leaves. These can be picked and added to salads, such as potato salads or savoury salad dishes with beetroot. The flavour is fresh and only mildly bitter if picked early in spring when the buds and leaves are tender. In addition, the leaves have a pleasant nutty taste, and you can also add the young buds to spring puddings. Alternatively, the leaves can be dried and brewed as a tea.

The young buds and leaves were once a favourite wild snack of children, which gave the Hawthorn its nickname of the bread-and-cheese tree. The bread-and-cheese has a nutty taste and can be eaten straight from the trees, picked for sandwiches, added to any recipe for wild spring greens and potatoes, added to spring puddings, or perhaps eaten with a plate of other nuts and cheese. Richard Mabey suggests:

> A sauce for spring lamb can be made by chopping the leaves with other early wild greens, such as garlic mustard and sorrel, and dressing with vinegar and brown sugar, as with a mint sauce.

An account by Mrs A. B of Cheshire (in 2002) says:

> Happy memories they are of eating bread-and-cheese on the way to school in the spring. As the Hawthorn hedge broke into tiny delicious leaves, we picked them gently not to get pricked by the thorns and enjoyed a second breakfast all the way to school.

Hawthorn was not only a popular wild edible; it was once a medicinal food in times past.

A few decades ago, elders in northern England still chewed regularly on a fresh leaf to strengthen the heart. There, the leaf was called old man's sandwich.

As a potential food source for commercial use, Hawthorn is listed by the Council of Europe as a natural source of food flavouring; if used in small doses.

Nutritionally, Hawthorn contains flavonoids with heart-friendly antioxidant activity (discussed later) and tannins, essential oils, fruit acids, and sugars.

Hawthorn also contains vitamins B and C. It is known as nutrition for the heart, being widely prescribed in herbal medicine for heart complaints. In some parts of Portugal, children were given haws to eat because of their high nutritional content.

Hawthorn Jelly Recipe

- 700g Hawthorn berries (haws)
- 850ml water
- 1 lemon (juiced) sugar

Wash the haws, then add them to a saucepan with a heavy bottom and cover with the water. Bring to a boil and slowly simmer for one hour. Mash the berries well with a potato masher every 20 minutes. When done, allow straining overnight through a jelly bag or muslin. To keep the jelly clear, do not squeeze the jelly bag; just let the juice drip. If you're not bothered whether your Hawthorn jelly is clear or not, then squeeze away.

For every 500ml of liquid, measure out 500g sugar. Juice the lemon and mix with the sugar in a heavy saucepan along with the Hawthorn juice. Bring to the boil stirring continuously until the sugar has dissolved, then rapid boil for 10 minutes or until the jelly has reached setting point. Skim off any foam from the top of the jelly liquid, and pour into sterilised, warm jars and screw on the lids.

Hawthorn Brandy Cordial

When the Hawthorn is in full bloom, pick a basketful of the flowers. Take them home, and put the white petals into a large glass bottle, taking care to exclude leaves or stalks. When the bottle is full to the top, do not press it down, but gently pour as much brandy as it will hold. Cork and let it stand for three months, then you can strain it off. This is good as a cordial, and if you find it too strong, add water, or sweeten it with sugar. (Circa 1915)

Hawthorn Tea

Pick fully opened young Hawthorn leaves, rinse in cold water. Place in a steamer and cook until the colour has changed from vibrant green to an olive colour. Heat a saucepan on high until it is scalding, then dry-toast the leaves stirring continuously until dry. Store in a jar for use in the same way you would make black tea.

Hawthorn Flower Syrup

- 5 cups of Hawthorn flowers (picked when they have pink stamens and smell sweet)
- caster sugar
- 800g granulated sugar
- 1.25 litres of water
- 6 tablespoons of lemon juice

Snip the flowers from the stalks and loosely put them in a large screw-top Kilner jar until they are 3cms deep, then sprinkle a small amount of caster sugar over them. Repeat, alternating the flowers with sugar until the jar is full. Do not compress the flowers. Next, put the water, granulated sugar and lemon juice into a pan and bring to a gentle simmer. Stir continuously until the sugar has melted (about 2-3 minutes). Take off the heat and allow the mixture to cool.

Pour the cooled syrup over the flowers, and loosely screw the lid on. Next, fold up some newspaper and place it in the bottom of a large saucepan. Stand the jar of Hawthorn flowers on top. Fill the pan up with cold water, then turn up the heat and simmer gently for an hour. Take the jars out of the pan, and screw the lids on firmly. Allow to go cold, then strain the flower syrup into a jug and pour into sterilised individual bottles and cap. Brown bottles are best. Store in a cool, dark place, and it will keep for months.

MEDICINE

As a magical tree, Hawthorn was often used for curing diseases through magical rituals. You can find stories of Hawthorn's healing power across Europe. In Slovakia, for example, a thorn from the tree was stuck deep into a facial wart as a cure. A variation on curing warts in Britain was to pass a slug or snail over the wart and then impaling the unfortunate creature on the thorns; the belief being as the slug or snail died, so too the wart would wither.

In southern Bavaria, as recently as 1940, a splinter of Hawthorn wood was stuck into a painful tooth until it bled to cure the toothache. The splinter was then returned to the tree. In Moravia, you inserted a strand of the person's hair into a Hawthorn tree to cure a fever. A variation of this cure in cattle was to hang the afterbirth of a calf on a Hawthorn to prevent the cow from getting a fever or, in other customs, ensure the herd's fertility for generations.

Magical cures that transferred the disease from the patient to the tree were not uncommon in plant lore, and Hawthorn is one of many rag or fetish trees. In Ireland, these thorny rag trees were often associated with sacred wells. In West Flanders, Belgium, a Hawthorn stood by Our Lord of the Tree chapel in Poperinge, a place of pilgrimage. People adorned the tree with all sorts of items from the sick in the hope of a cure. Another Hawthorn tree is said to serve as a nail tree where it stands in front of the 11th-century church of St Saviour in the Brabant village of Hakendover, Belgium.

During a procession on Easter Monday, pilgrims take a handful of earth from around the tree or a branch of the tree for its curative powers; such pilgrimages originated from Germanic field processions to make the fields more fertile. Today, the tree that stands by the chapel is said to be the descendant of the Hawthorn that grew there in 690AD.

A simple remedy for rheumatoid arthritis involved placing a Hawthorn twig under the patient's pillow. In Somerset, England, you would treat an infected wound with a Hawthorn charm. A thorn would be passed over the wound whilst reciting: 'Christ was of the Virgin born, He was prickled with a thorn, It never did hell and swell, I trust in Jesus this never will'.

In France, a patient who had a fever was told to take bread and salt to Hawthorn and say:

> *Adieu, buisson blanc; Je te porte du pain et du sel Et la fièvre pour demain.*
>
> *Farewell, white bush; I bring you bread and salt And fever for tomorrow.*

The bread was then fixed to a branch and the salt thrown over the tree. Then the patient would walk home on a different road to where he had come and used another door or window to enter his house. This custom was believed to transfer his fever to the tree.

Hawthorn has a long history of use in folk medicine as well as in magical healing. For example, Dioscorides recommended Hawthorn for relieving diarrhoea and preventing menstruation. Flemish herbalist Rembert Dodoens (Dodonaeus) and Dutch Abraham Munting prescribed a compress of Hawthorn roots to draw out splinters. Culpeper wrote:

> The seeds in the berries beaten to powder being drank in wine, are held singularly against the stone; and are good for the dropsy. The distilled water of the flowers stay the lask. The seed cleared from

the down, bruised and boiled in wine, and drank, is good for inward tormenting pains. If cloth or sponges be wet in the distilled water, and applied to any place wherin thorns or splinters, or the like, do abide in the flesh, it will notably draw them forth.

He adds: 'And thus you see the thorn gives a medicine for its own pricking, and so doth almost every thing else.'

John Gerard (1545–1612) wrote about the berries and seed:

> The Hawes or berries of the Hawthorne tree, as Dioscorides writeth, doe both stay the Laske, the menses, and all other fluxes of bloud. Some Authors write, that the stones beaten to pouder and giuen to drinke are good against the stone.

Watts also tells us that Hawthorn was a common remedy for stone: 'Of course, this may very well have been from the doctrine of signatures – the stone fruits to destroy the stone'.

Herbalist Salmon (1644–1713) wrote that the berries could cure fluxes and haemorraghes. The Gunton Household Book of the 17th and 18th centuries gave a recipe for a conserve made from Hawthorn berries to treat diabetes or a paste mixed with cider or wine to treat kidney stones.

There are numerous recipes for Hawthorn in herbal medicine. Hawthorn blossoms, for example, have been used for mild heart complaints. The tree has long provided a remedy for coronary heart disease, angina, high and low blood pressure, rapid pulse, irregular heartbeat, and even heart failure in herbal medicine. The ancient Celts used Hawthorn berries as a diuretic which is another way of treating heart complaints. However, they also used the berries to remedy a broken heart to remove sadness and anxiety.

Jackson tells us that the first mention of Hawthorn's effect on the heart is Quercetanus, personal physician of King Henry IV of France, who invented an anti-age syrup from the tree. The Scottish used Hawthorn to treat blood pressure, and in the Isle of Man and Devon, the flowers and berries are considered a heart tonic. In the Scottish Highlands, Hawthorn tea was drunk to balance high or low blood pressure. In Russia, healers treated angina with an infusion of Hawthorn fruits, and in Germany, they used an alcohol infusion.

The fruits are a popular remedy for stomach aches and diarrhoea, as mentioned in early European herbals. In addition, women took a compote of fresh fruits to relieve hot flushes during menopause.

In Irish folk medicine, the bark was steeped in black tea and the liquid used to treat toothache or burns. An Irish physician, Dr Green, in the 19th century, treated hundreds of patients with a secret remedy for angina, coronary thrombosis, palpitations, chest pains and other heart disorders. After his death, it was revealed the mixture to be a tincture of Hawthorn berries. The flowers or leaves were infused to treat sore throats in the Scottish Highlands and the Isle of Man.

Around the world, in folk medicine, African tribes used Hawthorn to treat rheumatism, and in China, people used it to treat stomach complaints; the blossoms and berries have been used in traditional Chinese medicine for thousands of years. The leaves, flowers, fruit and bark have also been used in traditional Chinese medicine to remedy heart disorders.

It was a favourite herb of Eclectic physician and author of The American Materia Medica, Finley Ellingwood, who said 'Hawthorn is superior to any other of the wellknown and tried remedies at present in use in the treatment of heart disease'.

Henriette Kress summarises Hawthorn as 'Stinky flowers, sharp spines, and mealy berries - but it's great for the heart'.

Recent pharmacological studies have confirmed that Hawthorn is effective in treating congestive heart failure.

While it doesn't contain digitalis-like components such as cardiotonic glycosides or cardiotonic alkaloids, it contains flavonoids that dilate blood vessels and effect blood pressure. Bartrams notes that Hawthorn may be helpful where digitalis is not tolerated. It includes a cornucopia of compounds. These compounds are again flavonoids that have antioxidant activity and help protect body cells by destroying free radicals.

Hawthorn also contains heart-friendly compounds. 'Procyanidins are beta blockers, and so calm down a heart that is beating erratically and make it beat steadily and rhythmically. Vitexin rhamnoside protects the heart cells deprived of oxygen and glucose.' The flavonoids, particularly the procyanidins, or proanthocyanidins (OPCs), are attributed by Yance, as the primary cardioprotective components of the plant. 'These flavonoids have very strong vitamin P activity, working synergistically to enhance the activity of vitamin C and promoting capillary stability.'

The plant tannins also slow the heart rate and make it beat stronger. The herb also has a mild sedative activity which can make it useful for symptoms of mild heart disease. The plant has been recommended for specific heart conditions such as right-heart failure, where the right side of the heart fails to pump blood efficiently.

From a herbalist's point of view, Kress recommends Hawthorn as a preventative or as a first line of defence against developing serious heart complaints, including:

- strengthens blood vessels and capillaries
- improves the heart muscle's oxygen uptake and helps it use the oxygen more efficiently
- slows the pulse (the heart beats slower)
- enhances coronary and myocardial blood
- calms and relaxes.

Newall and team (1996) record a commercial product containing Hawthorn, valerian, camphor, and cereus, which was given to 2,243 patients with cardiovascular disorders. They reported an improvement in 84% of individuals. Another commercial Hawthorn preparation was reportedly effective in treating sixty patients with angina.

Only trained herbalists or doctors can use the herb in doses high enough to be effective. 'Herbalists use it for mild heart failure, myocardial weakness, irregular heartbeat and palpitations.'

Yance cites two placebo-controlled trials for testing the use of this herb in patients with mild forms of heart failure, which reported both subjective and objective improvements. He adds that: 'other studies of Hawthorn in patients with heart failure have revealed improvement in clinical symptoms'. A randomised trial to demonstrate the hypotensive effects of Hawthorn in diabetes patients showed an improvement in their average diastolic blood pressure. Hawthorn may also be helpful for those who have heart problems caused by hepatitis or other liver diseases.

When taken after a heart attack, Hawthorn 'accelerates healing and improves the heart's oxygen uptake'. However, I would advise you not to self-medicate and seek the guidance of a professional medical herbalist.

The plant can strengthen collagen in the body, which enables it to heal damage to coronary arteries and valve deficiency; this activity may also make it worthwhile for haemorrhoids, sprains and varicose veins. While strengthening collagen may also affect skin firmness, its antioxidant activity could also have an age-related effect by reducing vascular inflammation.

Hawthorn may also strengthen connective tissue, being helpful for tears in tendons and ligaments or even for arthritis or rheumatism. It can calm people who are stressed, and a decoction of Hawthorn tea can relieve nervous energy if taken over a period of time. Eating Hawthorn sandwiches filled with the young leaves can increase concentration. Newall and team (1996) noted a mild depressant effect on the central nervous system in mice fed Hawthorn flower extracts.

James Duke recommends Hawthorn as a remedy for various ailments, including fatigue and insomnia, inflammations and swelling, and that the plant may be effective against certain cancers. In addition, Hawthorn, combined with ginkgo, can enhance poor memory by improving the blood-oxygen circulation to the brain.

Herbalists have also used several different species of Hawthorn since the late 1990s to treat people with asthma. This may be due to the anti-inflammatory and antiallergenic flavonoids in the plant. Some herbalists recommend Hawthorn as a decoction to gargle for sore throats, and the plant can treat some inner ear problems. When used regularly, Hawthorn is said to help withstand the summer heat.

The plant has been used as a medicinal food, combining healthy eating with its health-giving benefits. The fruits, for example, also have laxative and digestive properties, and the jam can be used as an anticatarrhal, which may be particularly helpful to eat during the hayfever season or during the winter to ease colds and flu. In addition, the Nlaka'pamux of Canada ate haws fresh and dried for diarrhoea and general sickness.

SAFETY NOTE

Pedersen notes that Hawthorn does not appear to be cardiotoxic as the herb does not have cumulative effects. However, toxicity has been reported at very high doses. While the berries are not sweet enough to appeal to children, haws may be poisonous if eaten in excess.

Conway comments that Hawthorn can help lower blood pressure and should be avoided in people with low blood pressure. Likewise, Newall and team (1996) advise Hawthorn should not be used to self-medicate by people with cardiac disorders given the plant's effects on the heart and blood pressure.

Mills and Bone also advise that Hawthorn should not be used simultaneously as taking prescribed cardiac or blood pressure medications.

The herb may initially cause heart palpitations in some, which should subside within one or two days of stopping treatment. Nevertheless, it would be sensible to report any adverse reactions to your health care professional.

There have been some cases of Hawthorn causing adverse reactions such as nausea, fatigue, sweating and rashes on hands, and that an overdose could be fatal. Therefore, pregnant or breastfeeding women should avoid the herb. However, other sources suggest that there have been no adverse effects caused by Hawthorn in pregnancy or breastfeeding; it is still best to exercise caution.

HAZEL
Corylus avellana

FAMILY

Betulaceae.

BOTANICAL DESCRIPTION

Height: up to 6–12 m. Flowers: male flowers show as one to four drooping catkins, female flowers show in erect, short spikes with red styles. Bark: smooth, reddish-brown peeling bark. Leaves: roundish, downy, toothed leaves. Fruit: a globose to ovoid nut enclosed within large, fused bracts.

FLOWERS

January to April.

STATUS

Perennial. Native.

HABITAT

Deciduous woodland, hedgerows, scrub.

OVERVIEW

Hazel was one of the first trees to colonise the land after the last Ice Age, and it would have been one of the most abundant tree species.

It is little wonder then that the Hazel tree has become deeply entrenched in our ancient history, beliefs and customs. Hazel forests provided materials for making houses, fences, furniture, baskets and tools. Its charcoal gave early people the thrill of gunpowder. The nuts provided a valuable source of sustenance probably since prehistory.

Storytellers told epic stories about the tree and its fruit (Hazelnuts) from ancient Greece to Medieval Europe, and people knew its magical reputation in many traditions. The theme of the Hazel was woven into wisdom, knowledge and poetry, which Hazelnuts, in particular, were believed to bestow upon humankind. Yet for all its vaunted power, in the language of flowers, Hazel signifies reconciliation and peace.

FOOD

The most common edible part of the tree is its nuts. Hazelnuts have been an essential part of human diets since the Stone Age. Archaeological excavations in Flanders, Belgium, uncovered evidence that Stone Age people, around c13,000 years ago, roasted Hazelnuts to store over winter. The Romans cultivated the nuts, and Pliny the Elder (23–79 AD) commented on nuts coming from Asia and being brought into Greece.

Aside from providing nutritionally rich fat, Hazelnuts have long been enjoyed as a sweet treat, and various tree species provide a recognised world food crop. According to de Cleene and Lejeune, Turkey, Italy, and Spain are currently the primary producers of Hazelnuts. Turkey produces 200,000 tons per annum, Spain 20,000 tons and Italy 50,000 tons; the US has 10,000 tons per annum. The Hazelnut is second only to the almond as a world nut crop. The best nuts are from Spain, called Barcelona nuts.

According to François Couplan, Hazelnuts contain 15% protein and are rich (60%) in fatty acids, vitamins and minerals, such as vitamins E and B (particularly B6), zinc, iron, calcium, potassium, selenium and magnesium. Richard Mabey writes: 'Weight for weight, they contain fifty per cent more protein, seven times more fat and five times more carbohydrate than hens' eggs.' TK Lim suggests that Hazelnuts are 'the second-best source of vitamin E after plant oils', an essential nutrient for muscle tissue and the reproductive system. With this in mind, Hazelnuts make an excellent vitamin and protein-rich nut cutlet.

Further, Hazelnuts are known to have one of the highest ORAC values (Oxygen Radical Absorbance Capacity), which definitely ranks them as a superfood. Foods with high ORAC values are considered helpful against free radicals or oxidisation of body cells that contribute to chronic illness and disease incidences. Hazelnuts score more highly on ORAC scales than almonds and pistachios, though not as high as pecans and walnuts.

As Culpeper might say, Hazelnuts are so well known that it hardly seems worthy to describe them as a wild edible. The nuts are extensively produced and sold by the food industry. You are undoubtedly familiar with nut butter, Hazelnut chocolate spreads and fillings for biscuits, cakes, pastries, desserts and sweets. Hazelnuts are also famously used in a paste to make praline, such as in Belgian chocolates. Lim writes: 'In Australia, Hazelnut is used in the manufacture of Cadbury eponymous milk chocolate bar which is the third most popular brand in Australia. In Austria, Hazelnut paste is an important ingredient in the world-famous torts (such as Viennese Hazelnut tort).' In the US, Hazelnuts are used in nut butter, considered more nutritious than the alternatives like peanut butter.

The kernels, too, are used in confectionery and sweetmeats. Simple recipes for Hazelnuts at home might include cookies, pies or add to cereals. The chopped nuts may be added to sauces or sprinkled over baked fish. In times past, Hazelnuts were not only a valuable source of nourishment, but an additional income for local people.

> At Ashmore and other villages on Cranborne Chase [Dorset] the annual nutting expeditions were great events. The women and girls made themselves special canvas dresses and the great part of the population went off to the woods, taking their 'nammit' (noonmeat) with them. The nuts were sold to dealers for dessert and also (chiefly) for use in the dyeing industry. Often not less than £200 a year was made by the village during this season, and most families reckoned to pay their whole year's rent, if nothing more, with the proceeds. This custom has now almost come to an end. There is now little sale for the nuts to dyers, and very low prices prevailed in the years between the two great wars so the nutting ceased to be worthwhile. During the wars prices rose again and 6d a lb for slipped nuts was obtained between 1939 and 1945. The price has now fallen to 4d a lb, and during the last decade, it is only the children and the old people who have troubled to carry on the work.
>
> — DACOMBE, 1951

There, a brief history of nutting and how a seemingly humble wild edible contributed to local traditions and livelihoods. Even after the practice ceased to be profitable, carefree nutting expeditions continued in the countryside. However, people remained aware of the dangers of nutting on a Sunday and bumping into the devil.

> *Oh, there was a maid, and a foolish young maid,*
> *And she went a-nutting on Sunday.*
> *She met with a Gentleman all in black,*
> *He took her, and he laid her a-down on her back,*
> *All a-cause she went nutting on Sunday.*

Thus nutting was also a euphemism for secret trysts and couple's lovemaking.

If you'd like to collect Hazelnuts, seasoned foragers suggest searching inside bushes, giving them a shake, using a walking stick to pull down branches, and gathering the nuts into a basket, all the while being aware that you are competing with the birds and squirrels. Of course, if you come across a squirrel's stash, it seems a little mean-spirited to steal it. Nevertheless, a bowl of Hazelnuts is always a welcome treat come Christmas Day too.

The food industry has made less use of the yellow, edible oil extracted from Hazelnuts because it turns rancid quickly and has a short shelf life. But it is suitable for drizzling on salads and as a frying oil or spread on bread as an alternative to butter. It, of course, has a delicious nutty aroma and taste. The seeds also provide edible oil. The kernels contain 18% protein and 68% oil, which is sometimes sold commercially and may be used like olive oil. Hazelnut oil is rich in vitamin E as well as beneficial fatty acids. You may use the residual meal from the oil extraction to make a gluten-free flour.

The leaves of the tree were of importance too. In the 15th century, Hazel leaves were used in a recipe to make noteye, a spicy pork stew. The leaves were ground and mixed with ginger, saffron, sugar, salt, and vinegar before adding to minced pork. People dried and ground Hazel leaves to make flour for biscuits and bread in 18th-century Scotland.

In Turkey, the leaves are used to wrap sarmas, which is usually a filling of mincemeat. The nutshells are used as fuel and to colour wine. In Egypt, ground Hazelnuts are mixed with olive oil in a spice blend, dukka, used for dipping bread. In Estonia in spring, raw catkins of Hazel were once stamped to add to bread dough when other crops were scarce. In Kazan, Russia, Hazelnuts are very plentiful, and the expressed oil is used in food. Hazelnut milk is processed into Hazelnut liqueurs with a vodka base in Eastern Europe and North America.

The kernels of the American Hazel (*C. americana*) may be eaten raw or added to soups, bread, cookies, and cakes. Stephen Facciola writes: 'Indians of the prairie regions preferred them in the milk stage when they are softer and sweeter.' The nuts of two American species – *C. americana* and *C. cornuta* were eaten by natives tribes, including the Omaha, Ponca, Winnebago, Potawatomi, and Dakota. The Iroquois cooked Hazelnut meats, ground the nuts to mix in flour for bread and puddings or boiled them to skim off the oil for use with other foodstuffs. The Okanagan-Colville tribe ate the kernels with bear oil, meat or grease, cooked them with berries and roots, or made them into cakes.

Hazelnut and Seaweed Loaf

- 200g sOaked Hazelnuts
- 50g sOaked sunflower seeds
- 1 fresh red chilli (chopped)
- 50g fresh flat leaf parsley (chopped)
- 20g dried seaweed flakes
- 2 tbsp tamari
- 2 tbsp olive oil
- 4 eggs

SOak the nuts and seeds overnight, then strain and run fresh water through them. Allow to sit for 60 minutes, then add to a food processor and pulse until they become a meal (finely chopped). Add the chopped chilli and parsley, add the seaweed flakes, tamari and olive oil and pulse again until thoroughly mixed. Spoon into a bowl. Beat the eggs well, then add to the mixture and stir well.

Grease a loaf tin, spoon in the mix and bake in the oven for 30 minutes on 400°F/200°C/180° Fan.

Hazelnut and Wild Garlic Pâté

- 200g dried cashews
- 30g wild garlic leaves
- ½ tsp sea salt
- 2 tbsp raw apple cider vinegar
- 2 tbsp of sauerkraut juice (optional)

SOak Hazelnuts for 4 hours in tepid water and a pinch of salt. Drain and place into a food processor and pulse into a chunky paste. Add the chopped wild garlic leaves, sea salt, cider vinegar and sauerkraut juice. Pulse until smooth. Scrape out into a cheesecloth and wring out as much liquid as possible. Leave the mixture in a tightened cheesecloth inside a sieve over a jug. Allow to sit for 3 hours, then put in a jar or storage container, cap and place in the fridge. Let it mature for two days, then eat. Should keep for seven days if kept refrigerated.

MEDICINE

The Hazel tree was a powerful magical healer. For example, in Wallonia in Belgium, people placed a hollow Hazelnut filled with mercury in sachets on a patient's chest to cure them. Dioscorides might not have used this particular charm, but he said that Hazel cured coughing; he considered it bad for the stomach. Finding double Hazelnuts was again considered very fortunate as you could use them to cure people of toothache, rheumatism and witch's curses.

The renowned German mystic Hildegard of Bingen (1098–1179) mentioned Hazelnuts and peppers to cure male infertility but adds that the remedy will only work if God is willing. Overall, she did not rate the Hazel much in healing and said it would not harm those who are well but should be avoided by those who are ill. Flemish herbalist Rembert Dodoens (1517–1585), or Dodonaeus, was similarly cautious about the Hazel in medicine:

> Hazelnuts are not very nutritious and difficult to digest; they cause flatulence in the stomach and headaches if too many are eaten. Hazelnuts consumed with a drink of mead cure old coughs, and if roasted and eaten with a little pepper are good for catarrh.

English herbalist John Gerard (1545–1612) was less reserved about using Hazel:

> The kernels of Nuts made into Milk like Almonds, doth mightily binde the belly, and is good for the laske and the bloody fluxe. The same doth coole exceedingly in hot fevers, and burning agues.

He added that oil from the tree's wood was 'reported to be very good against the Epilepsie and other Disease of the Head and Brain.'

We find much praise for the Hazel as a medicinal plant in the English herbalist Nicholas Culpeper's Complete Herbal of 1653:

> They are under the dominion of mercury. The parted kernels made into an electuary, or the milk drawn from the kernels with mead or honeyed water, is very good to help in old cough; and being parched, and a little pepper put to them and drank, digest the distillations of rheum from the head. The dried husks and shells, to the weight of two drams; taken in red wine, stays lasks and women's courses; and so doth the red skin that covers the kernels, which is more effectual to stay women's courses.

He then puzzles over complaints by 'the vulgar' that Hazel causes shortness of breath, to which he responds 'nothing is falser'. Culpeper defends the Hazelnut, which he claims strengthens the lungs and makes 'an apology for Nuts; which cannot speak for themselves.' Dutch herbalist Abraham Munting (1626–1683) agreed Hazelnuts were good for the lungs and for ailments of the head and limbs:

> Crushed and eaten with currants or raisins, they relieve the old cough and are good for the lungs. The ash of Hazelnuts mixed with vinegar and oil prevent hair-loss and cures head scabies if applied to the head. Hazelnut oil is good for painful limbs and the gout.

Old medicinal remedies for Hazel included brewing catkin-tea for colds and flu, decocting the bark for fever, and taking the leaves for diarrhoea. While the tree had great spiritual importance in Ireland, Hatfield notes only a few records for Hazel in folk medicine: the bark treated cuts and boils, and the ashes used to treat burns.

In veterinary folk medicine, farmers tied Hazel branches to the legs of a horse who had overeaten, and a formula whispered in the animal's ear to cure its symptoms.

The Hazel has been a useful tree worldwide in folk medicine, though largely its uses were reserved for magic by early people. *C. americana*, the American cousin of *C. avellana*, provided fresh nuts for Iroquois women to give them strength during pregnancy. In India, people used oil derived from the seeds of *C. jacquemontii* to relieve sore muscles.

Hazel leaves are still sometimes used in modern herbalism to stimulate blood circulation and bile secretion. The latter might be why the leaves are included in remedies for liver and gall bladder complaints. The nut of Hazel is considered a tonic for the stomach.

Although the tree is not overly used in herbalism, the bark, leaves, catkins and nuts are all considered to be astringent, haemostatic, vasoconstrictive, blood purifying, fever-fighting, sweat-inducing and odontalgic – the latter relating to toothache, and perhaps referring to Hazel's early use as a charm to relieve toothache. Hazel oil is considered vasoconstrictive and might be helpful for varicose veins, haemorrhoids and internal bleeding. It's sometimes used to fight threadworm and pinworm in young children because of its gentle action.

In the cosmetic industry, Hazelnut oil is a nourishing ingredient in body and hand creams, lotions, soaps and face masks. In addition, extracts from the oil have been used in shampoos, balsams, and suntan oils.

In scientific research, extracts of *C. avellana* have been found to contain antibacterial components. Hazelnut extracts demonstrate antimicrobial activity against bacteria, such as *Staphylococcus aureas*, or the so-called MRSA superbug. In addition, the leaf and shell extracts of *C. avellana* may have the ability to inhibit the development of cancerous tumours, thanks to an agent it contains called paclitaxel. Lim suggests: 'Large quantities of Hazelnut shell are found as discarded material from food industries and provide good sources of taxane compounds of paclitaxel and other antineoplastic compounds.'

SAFETY NOTE

At present, there are no known contraindications or drug interactions to taking Hazel as a medicinal plant. Allergic reactions to the nuts and pollen of Hazel have been reported. In Europe, Hazelnuts are a frequent cause of food allergies, which is unsurprising considering the vast number of foods that include Hazelnuts, kernels and the oil in their ingredients. Allergies to Hazelnut can start at a young age and can be severe. People who suffer from nut allergies should avoid Hazelnuts and products containing nuts and nut oil.

HORSERADISH
Armoracia rusticana

FAMILY

Brassicaceae.

BOTANICAL DESCRIPTION

Stems 60-90 cms high, erect ; leaves on long stalks, 15-30 cms long, and 10-15 cms broad, sinuate and toothed at the edges, glabrous but rough, the lower stem leaves often deeply toothed, almost pinnatifid; flowers small, white, in numerous racemes, forming a terminal panicle; pods ovoid or elliptical.

FLOWERS

May to June.

STATUS

Perennial. Introduced.

HABITAT

Cultivated land, grassland, wasteland.

OVERVIEW

Horseradish has been cultivated since ancient times. It is thought to be indigenous to parts of eastern Europe, with several authorities saying it originated in southern Russia and Ukraine.

Other sources suggest it came to Britain as a spice plant from the Middle East in the 16th century or that its true origins are lost in time.

De Candolle (1959) supported the theory that Horseradish originated in temperate eastern Europe because it grew from 'Finland and Poland to the Caspian Sea and the deserts of Cuman and in Turkey,' but became more scattered towards western Europe.

Its most primitive name, chren, was common in Slavic languages, which later became kren, kreen, and cran in old German and French dialects.

Recorded history is not always constant, which is undoubtedly the case for Horseradish. Possibly the plant was known to Pliny (23–79AD), Roman naturalist and philosopher, as Armoracia, which was cultivated for medicinal use. However, Dioscorides of Greece (40–90AD) and Pliny also listed Horseradish as Thlaspi or Persicon.

Other sources doubt that Horseradish is the same plant as Armoracia because it is not mentioned in other ancient texts. For example, in 16th-century Italy, it is found again under the title of Armoracia but not described.

Interestingly, Armoracia is similar to an ancient name for Britain – Armorica – where Horseradish has grown wild for centuries.

Horseradish entered the Materia Medica of the 18th-century London Pharmacopoeia as *Raphanus rusticanus*. Mrs Grieve wrote that the Greeks called a wild radish *Raphanos agrios*, and Richard le Strange suggests that there could be a connection between the two plants.

A wild and domesticated plant, like Horseradish, was described in the 13th century by Albertus Magnus (1200–1280) called Raphanus. However, Carl Linnaeus (1707–1778), the Swedish botanist who developed the modern uniform system for naming species, changed the plant's Latin name to *Cochlearia armoracia*. Cochleare was an old-fashioned name for a spoon, which must have seemed fitting to Linnaeus because the leaves are spoon-shaped. Horseradish has since been reclassified as *Armoracia rusticana*.

The English name Horseradish means coarse radish from the prefix horse, distinguishing it from the garden radish (*R. sativus*), a practice used to describe other wild plants such as horse mint and horse chestnut.

According to Geoffrey Grigson, the first mention of the common name Horseradish in print appears in the works of English herbalist John Gerard (1545-1612). However, Gerard did not have much familiarity with the plant.

The German name for Horseradish was Meerettich, meaning sea radish; meer may derive from mähre, or old horse, in reference to its tough roots.

The French name was raifort, meaning strong root, or moutarde des moines, meaning monks mustard.

In many herbal texts, Horseradish is a garden escapee because it prefers growing alongside roads, wastelands and neglected places. However, it belongs to the cruciferous (mustard) vegetable family, which includes broccoli, cabbage and cauliflower, and has been used as a spice for over 2,000 years.

It's sold for quite a high price when one considers you can pick it in the wild in abundance. But do remember that UK law requires the landowner's permission before collecting any wild plant roots.

FOOD

Horseradish is one of the five bitter herbs eaten at the Jewish Feast of Passover, including coriander, horehound, lettuce, and nettle. The bitter herbs represent the suffering of the Jewish people's ancestors during the exodus from Egypt. In ancient times, people also used bitter, spicy herbs to disguise the taste and smell of spoiled meat.

As an aside, Mark Pedersen suggests the plant's irritant effect on mucous membranes may have had a beneficial impact on past diets. If you were eating spoiled meat regularly, Horseradish would irritate the mucous membranes of your digestive tract into producing a protective mucous coat that could prevent further irritation, inflammation, nausea and possibly absorb some of the putrefied substances in the meat.

Britain was unfamiliar with Horseradish as a culinary herb in the Middle Ages because its use was largely reserved for medicine. Still, herbalists were aware that it was a popular condiment in Germany and Denmark. Gerard wrote:

> The Horse Radish stamped with a little vinegar put thereto, is commonly used among the Germans for sauce to eate fish with and such like meates as we do mustarde.

Half a century later, the British had begun to acquire a taste for Horseradish, but it was not for the faint of heart. The herbalist John Parkinson (1567–1650) wrote that it was eaten by 'country people and strong labouring men in some countries of Germany... and in our owne land also, but...it is too strong for tender and gentle stomaches.'

As its use increased among country folk, Horseradish was found growing by inns and coach stations to use for travellers.

The fresh roots are used as a culinary seasoning, either as a sauce, powder or vinegar for flavouring meats, vegetables and pickles.

The herb is available in white (preserved in vinegar) or red (preserved in beet juice), although it is most famous for accompanying roast beef, steaks and smoked fish.

After washing and peeling the outer brown layer, the white inner root is grated with cream, vinegar, mustard and seasonings. The flavour of the sauce can be overpoweringly hot for some and so use sparingly.

Peter Wyse Jackson mentions Horseradish vinegar as an alternative relish for cold beef. You can also mix it with tomato sauce or tomatoes (as is done in Russia) to accompany seafood. In Alsace, France, a warm version of Horseradish root with fresh cream is prepared. The roots can be sliced and roasted as a vegetable. In Germany, sliced Horseradish roots are cooked like parsnips.

In his Culinary Herbs, Ernest Small warns that slicing Horseradish roots can produce a 'penetrating odour' causing 'extreme tearing or even nausea.' So remember to open the kitchen window or door if you're preparing Horseradish roots at home.

The young leaves have a pleasant flavour and can be added to salads, pickles or cooked as a potherb; the larger leaves can taste like cabbage and are more spicy and bitter. Herbalists suggest adding the leaves in smaller quantities if unsure about the flavour. In addition, you can add the sprouted seeds to season salads. Fish fillets baked with Horseradish and sour cream, Horseradish cranberry jelly, and Horseradish bloody Mary are among the many imaginative ways to use the plant.

One source suggests adding the acrid-tasting plant to vegetable curries and bakes. It also goes well with sausages, chicken, eggs, asparagus, avocado, beets, carrots, potatoes, turnips, and coleslaw. It has a particular affinity with apple, beetroot, and dill.

Wiersema and León list Horseradish as a world economic plant, and it's widely used as a food ingredient around the world. Horseradish is among the few wild plants still gathered in Poland with the roots and leaves prepared as a seasoning and preservative. The Polish mix Horseradish with beets to make a traditional condiment called cwikla for sausage and ham served at Easter.

The roots can be added to pickled cucumbers, soups, egg or meat dishes as a seasoning. The leaves are placed under baked bread to prevent it from sticking to the pan and to season the dough. In Belarus, *A. rusticana* is used to make local delicacies such as a spicy paste called kren, used to spice up fermented sauerkraut, cucumbers and tomatoes, and soups.

Forest plants used in Estonia for jams, condiments and beverages list Horseradish as a condiment. In Slovakia, it was a traditional famine plant used to spice meats; it may have been fermented in milk before boiling.

In Italy, the leaves are added to salads with other greens. In Transylvania, Horseradish is mixed with red beet as a salad called sfecla cu hrean served with lamb at Easter.

In Russia, Bulgaria and Romania, minced or grated Horseradish root is mixed with various ingredients such as vinegar, cream, oil, tomato and flavouring to make a sauce or relish for fish dishes or meat appetisers. The whole root may be chopped or grated for pickling vinegar to preserve cabbage; both roots and leaves can be used in pickling different vegetables, including carrots and peppers.

It has been a particular delicacy in Romania. The grated roots are eaten with potatoes or polenta or mixed with cream to serve with lamb or chicken; a tasty mix of Horseradish, apples, vinegar, salt and sugar makes a traditional garnish; and pieces of the roots added to a soup.

Giulio and his team (2016) investigated the diversity of vegetable crops in Romania, including locally adapted and cultivated species. They found *A. rusticana* used in local cuisine to flavour grilled meats and other traditional dishes.

Romanians also use the leaves to wrap meat, rice and vegetables in a boiled dish called sarmale, or add the leaves to bread dough and grill. In Romania and Bulgaria, Horseradish leaves are used as a fermenting agent to prepare alcohols; in Romania, they are added in the preparation of tuica, a fruit brandy.

A similar recipe called Apfelkren is prepared in Austria using freshly grated Horseradish with grated sour apples and served with meat.

In North America and southern Canada, where Horseradish in naturalised, the root is used as a condiment and the young leaves as a potherb. Early settlers brought Horseradish to the Americas and used to grow it outside cabins. However, it soon escaped and is considered a troublesome weed to some.

Dried Horseradish is sold commercially from Sweden and the US. It retains its spicy flavour and requires only water to rehydrate it.

Nevertheless, the sale of commercial Horseradish has declined in the US, and, according to Small, commercial crops can be inferior because the volatiles oils deteriorate in fresh preparations. Therefore, there is good reason to grow one's own.

In Japan, powdered Horseradish root is used to adulterate wasabi powder. However, the plant is said to be rare in China and not commonly used.

Nutritionally, Horseradish oil is rich in vitamin C (almost double per 100g as orange juice) with B vitamins, vitamin K, calcium, fibre, iron, potassium and protein.

The level of vitamin C in Horseradish is so high its effects on scurvy were considered miraculous, even when people dug the roots from the ground in winter. Indeed the plant is considered to be most pungent in cold weather and best picked after the first frost.

Small writes: 'Some of the most potent Horseradish produced commercially comes from the region of Tuli Lakes, California, where there is frost every month of the year.'

As a cruciferous vegetable, Horseradish may have beneficial antioxidant properties. However, the plant loses much of its nutritional content when it is cooked. Its vitamin C denatures and nutrients like vitamin K, and calcium are cut by a half; cooking also removes the plant's pungency, as do long periods of refrigeration after preparation.

In other uses, some Horseradishes are grown for their ornamental leaves; gardeners can spray an infusion of the leaves onto apple trees to prevent brown rot; kept on the borders of vegetable patches, it can help grow healthy disease-resistant potatoes. In addition, the volatile oils in Horseradish may be an effective insecticide.

How To Preserve Wild Horseradish Root

- 130g fresh wild Horseradish root
- 150ml organic cider vinegar

Grate your Horseradish root in a food processor. The fumes are very strong and can be overpowering. Immediately spoon into a jar, then pour over the cider vinegar and store in a refrigerator. Makes: 130g and should keep for about a year.

Horseradish & Ground Ivy Mayonnaise

- 15g fresh ground ivy leaves and stems
- 1 egg (can we take free-range as a given please)
- 200 ml rapeseed oil
- 3 tsp grated Horseradish root
- 2 tbsp lemon juice

Add egg to a hand blender jug, along with 150ml of oil and lemon juice. Blitz until thick, if too thin add more oil. Add chopped ground ivy and Horseradish root, then blitz until blended into the mayo. Serve with beef, or as a coleslaw type of dressing.

Horseradish Leaf Bubble and Squeak

- 600g floury potatoes such as Maris Piper or King Edwards
- 120g Horseradish leaves, stalk removed and washed
- 1 small onion
- 30g butter
- Salt and pepper
- Olive oil and butter for frying

Peel the potatoes and cut into even-sized pieces. Bring to the boil in salted water and simmer for 15 minutes until just tender. Drain and leave to go cold, uncovered. Breaking them up roughly speeds the process. Cook the Horseradish leaves in 1cm salted water for 2 minutes until tender. Tip into a sieve and quickly cool under cold running water to stop cooking and retain the colour. Squeeze out the excess water, then spread out on a clean tea towel and leave to dry out thoroughly.

Finely chop the onion and fry for 5 minutes in the butter until softened but not browned. Mash the potatoes and chop the Horseradish into small pieces. Mix the potatoes, Horseradish and onion with buttery juices together and season well with salt and pepper. Shape the mixture into 8-10cm discs. I use a plain cutter to achieve a good crisp shape, but hands work just as well. Cover and chill for at least an hour. At this stage they could also be frozen and cooked at a later date.

To cook heat a large frying pan over a medium heat, add oil and butter and fry them for 5 minutes on each side when they should be crisp and golden brown. Serves: 4-5

MEDICINE

Horseradish is an ancient healing herb known to many civilisations and cultures since the days of the Pharaohs in 1500BC. Greek physicians recommended the warming plant as a back rub. In Medieval Europe, healers prepared the roots and leaves for troublesome inflammations, wounds and infections.

In Irish folk medicine, Horseradish treated inflammatory conditions such as rheumatism. It eased the pain of toothache if 'a piece of the root was put onto the gum near the painful tooth.'

The famous German abbess Hildegard of Bingen (1098–1179) described Horseradish's virtues as warm under the old medicine doctrines. She prescribed its use to strengthen the body or to cure pains in the heart or lung.

The sulphur-rich root was valued for increasing blood circulation in the skin. English physician Nicholas Culpeper (1616–1654) wrote: 'If bruised and laid to a part grieved with the sciatica, gout, joint-ache or hard swellings of the spleen and liver, it doth wonderfully help them all.'

The root was believed to be a diuretic that could be used as a reliable remedy for sciatica, gout, and stones in the body. Gipsies soaked fresh scrapings of the root in vinegar and used it as a poultice on the affected body parts. Gerard wrote: 'it mitigateth and asswageth the paine of hip or haunch, commonly called Sciatica.' All three virtues – reducing swellings, increasing blood flow, and promoting urination – were thought helpful to rheumatic conditions, for which this plant was often used.

In Wales, Horseradish was taken internally for rheumatism after it had been infused in a bottle of whiskey that had been buried in the ground for nine days. The Irish preferred Horseradish in malt whisky to cure pleurisy.

In Russia, Horseradish was mixed with paraffin and rubbed on parts of the body affected by rheumatism. A Romanian folk cure for rheumatism was Horseradish roots grated in warm milk and drunk in the morning before breakfast.

William Cole (1626–1662), an English herbalist and botanist, recommended Horseradish to expel worms from the body, particularly in children: 'Of all things given to children for worms, Horseradish is not the least, for it soon killeth and expelleth them.' Up until the late 20th century, Horseradish root was boiled and eaten to cure worms in parts of Britain.

The strong vaporous odour of the root, when broken, was used to banish heavy colds; so strong is the smell of cut Horseradish root that some find it more overbearing than cut onions.

Healers made a cough medicine from boiled Horseradish water in East Anglia. In Ireland, people used it for bronchial conditions, and like many plants in folk medicine, it had several other uses.

A remedy for lumbago in the Fens involved mixing grated Horseradish with boiling water and applying it to the sufferer's back before bedtime. This often caused a blister that people treated by removing the Horseradish plaster then baked in the oven until powdery. Finally, the Horseradish powder, with flour, was dusted over the person's back blister to complete the treatment.

Fenlanders also used Horseradish to treat stomach cramps, stop bleeding, and seal wounds. Eating three Horseradish leaves daily was a means of causing an abortion in the Fens.

In other parts of Britain, people rubbed the leaves on the skin to soothe nettle stings because they resembled dock leaves. Horseradish was even considered an aphrodisiac. Among the more outlandish claims was that wearing it around the neck deterred the plague and that sniffing the plant cured baldness.

A community of Germans from Russia were said to use Russian sauerkraut, which contained Horseradish as a seasoning, for treating influenza and liver disease. In Russian folk medicine, Horseradish (sometimes with mustard) was applied as a compress on the calves of both legs to cure insomnia; the reasoning for this is not explained. It may have remedied those restless legs, perhaps, that sometimes keep one awake. Freshly grated Horseradish in lemon juice was another Russian remedy to treat asthma.

It was known as a herbal healer to Native American Indians. The Cherokees used it to promote menstruation, relieve rheumatism, treat urinary stones, improve digestion, and remedy colds and asthma. The tribes of Ontario and Delaware made a leaf poultice for neuralgia, and the Mohegans used a leaf poultice to treat toothache. The Iroquois infused the root to treat diabetes.

Mrs Grieve recommends it 'taken with oily fish or rich meat, either by itself or steeped in vinegar, or in a plain sauce, it acts as an excellent stimulant to the digestive organs, and as a spur to complete digestion.' Eaten at frequent intervals throughout the day may get rid of a persistent cough.

Bartrams writes that Horseradish can raise the vital force in the elderly, aid digestion, and stimulate circulation. As a warming herb, it's beneficial for poor circulation, hypothermia, frostbite, chilblains, rheumatic joints, colds, flu and as a cure for fever.

The grated roots or leaves can be mixed with alcohol or vinegar and put in a cloth to apply externally to relieve pains. The roots are mixed with wine, a method also used in eastern Europe to relieve headaches and rheumatic pain. Freshly scraped Horseradish can even relieve facial neuralgia if held in the hand of the affected side. 'The hand in some cases within a short time becoming bloodlessly white and benumbed,' wrote Grieve.

Its remedy for chilblains is simple – the grated root was wrapped around the finger or toe and kept in place with a piece of lint. A poultice of Horseradish root can be used instead of a mustard plaster. You can take Horseradish syrup for a hoarse throat; the juice diluted in water with glycerine is said to relieve whooping cough in children.

Its expectorant effects may help treat respiratory diseases. For example, breathing problems and sinusitis are supposedly relieved by rubbing Horseradish paste on the throat.

A simple remedy for coughs and bronchitis is to mix Horseradish with honey from the black locust tree (*Robinia pseudoacacia*). Romanians are said to take a tablespoon of this mixture each morning for good health and to cure stomach problems.

In the Basilicata region of southern Italy, Horseradish leaves and roots are a traditional remedy for rheumatism, sinusitis, headaches, coughs and bronchitis. The plant is also an ingredient in a hangover remedy with dill, bay, and pickled tomatoes.

Indeed, Duke indicates Horseradish for many ailments, including anorexia, allergies; infrequent menstruation; certain cancers; diabetes, chilblains, congestion, catarrh, worms, wounds, toothache fungal infections, sore throats, kidney and urinary stones, and water retention.

Horseradish is sometimes included in herbal formulas to stimulate the immune system by increasing white blood cells. A herbal remedy to reduce blood pressure was to combine Horseradish roots with vinegar, salt and sugar.

The British Pharmacopoeia provides an official preparation for Horseradish taken as an extract with wine for chronic rheumatism. An infusion of Horseradish root infused in wine stimulates the nervous system and promotes perspiration.

Among its active constituents are coumarins, phenols, volatile oils and various other constituents such as ascorbic acid and enzymes.

Newall, Anderson and Phillipson write: 'The chemistry of Horseradish is well established and it is recognised as one of the richest plant sources of peroxidase enzymes.' This may support its use as a circulatory stimulant and wound healer, although more research is needed.

In Canada, Horseradish is grown for an enzyme peroxidase used to diagnose the AIDS virus. It has also been used to test blood glucose levels and to study rheumatoid arthritis. In addition, the enzyme is being researched as a potential new agent for anticancer therapies.

The component allyl isothiocyanate, found in many cruciferous vegetables, including Horseradish, has been shown to inhibit the growth of pancreatic cancer cells in laboratory testing.

Mucete and team (2006) studied the bioactivity of an important class of compounds in Horseradish, called glucosinolates, secondary plant metabolites with potential commercial applications within chemistry and food industries. The authors concluded that the active compounds in Horseradish exhibited effective antimicrobial activity against *E. coli*, *C. albicans*, and *S. aureus* by inhibiting their growth.

Marzocco and team (2015) looked at the anti-inflammatory activity of Horseradish extracts. Their research found its rich glucosinolates breakdown into other compounds, such as sulphur, that provide the plant's characteristic flavour and odour. The authors concluded that Horseradish has a protective effect on cells during inflammation and helps to prohibit inflammatory conditions.

Balasinska and team (2005) found that Horseradish did indeed lower blood cholesterol and bile secretion in mice fed a cholesterol-rich diet with Horseradish.

SAFETY NOTE

Horseradish is generally considered a safe herb by the US Food and Drug Administration (FDA); in the US, the herb is listed as GRAS (Generally Regarded As Safe). It's approved by Commission E for use in catarrh of the respiratory tract, urinary tract infections and to relieve minor muscular aches by improving blood flow. The Council of Europe list Horseradish as a food flavouring and it can be safely added to foods in small quantities.

However, caution is advised. Karalliedde and Gawarammana warn excessive doses can cause inflammation. In addition, caution is advised as frequent handling of the root may cause skin irritation, even blistering in sensitive individuals. It has also been observed that Horseradish produces heat when mixed with water due to chemical reactions that may cause sensitivity in some.

According to some authorities, Horseradish can depress thyroid function or may even lead to an enlarged thyroid gland and should not be used by those suffering from thyroid disease.

Karalliedde and Gawarammana record that it's contraindicated in chronic nephritis, hepatitis, gastro-oesophageal reflux, hyper-acidity conditions and in inflammatory bowel disease. Thus any condition in which the digestive system is sensitive or already compromised.

Duke writes that excessive use of Horseradish can lead to diarrhoea and night sweats. Gardner and McGuffin report there are no known contraindications to using Horseradish with other drugs or supplements.

The Commission E recommends Horseradish isn't taken by children under four years old, although there is no supporting evidence for this.

Some texts noted its abortifacient effects, which suggest it should be avoided in pregnancy as a precaution. The essential oil of Horseradish is reportedly hazardous and should not be used externally or internally.

Gardner and McGuffin, on the other hand, find no evidence to suggest Horseradish is hazardous during pregnancy, although its safety has not been completely established.

OAK
Quercus robur

FAMILY

Fagaceae.

BOTANICAL DESCRIPTION

This majestic-looking tree has wide-spreading, branches on a short, stout trunk. The bark is brown-grey and the leaves are dark green on top and pale blue-green beneath. The tree bears male and female flowers – male flowers are slender catkins and female flowers are globe-shaped and pale brown. The easily recognisable fruit – acorns – resemble a small nut inside a stalked cup.

FLOWERS

April to May.

STATUS

Perennial. Native.

HABITAT

Deciduous woodland, hedgerows.

OVERVIEW

From the Oak forests of Europe to the tropics of the Americas, around 500–600 species of Oak can be found. The Oak covered one third of Europe during the reign of England's King Henry VII (1457–1509), but these ancient forests have all but vanished due to logging.

Of all the mighty Oaks in the world, the English Oak or common Oak (*Quercus robur*), also called the Pedunculate Oak, Brown Oak, Truffle Oak or European Oak, is of particular importance to European mythology and it is *Q. robur* that is described here unless otherwise indicated.

Along with the ash and yew, which had great significance to the mother goddesses, the Oak was an important figure of the father gods and took its place among the supreme trees used in magic and ritual.

Oak is both a humble tree and a royal figure that has inspired humans throughout the ages with its steadfast trunk and widely outstretched branches. It was at once the tree of kings and a tree of peasants.

King Arthur's round table was said to be made from a single slice of Oak, while at the same time children in Ireland would catch a falling Oak leaf for good luck. Oak's unique story in plant lore was as the great patriarch of the forest.

FOOD

Acorns have long been valued as a special food - a gift from the Oak gods. The ancient Greeks considered the Oak to be the first tree that fell to earth to bring mankind the riches of acorns and honey.

While some classic authors described early inhabitants of Greece and southern Europe, living in primeval forests, as being fat on the fruits of the Oak. Folkard tells us: "These primitive people were called *Balanophagi* (eaters of Acorns)".

An English chronicler wrote in the 17th century:

Acorns...(before the use of Wheat-Corn was found out) were heretofore the Food of Men, nay of Jupiter himself ... till their Luxurious Palats were debauched ... And Men had indeed Hearts of Oak; I mean, not so hard, but health, and strength, and liv'd naturally, and with things easily parable and plain.

J Russell Smith suggests that historically humans may have eaten more acorns than wheat and that acorns were of great importance to hunter-gatherers, before the era of agriculture:

> ... for wheat is the food of only one of the four large masses of humans, the European-North American group. The other three groups, the Chinese-Japanese, the Indian (Asiatic), and the tropical peoples, pay small attention to wheat; hundreds of millions of their people have never heard of it. Meanwhile those humans (and possibly pre-humans) who dwelt in or near the Oak forests in the middle latitudes - Japan, China, Himalaya Mountains, West Asia, Europe, North America - have probably lived in part on acorns for unknown hundreds of centuries, possibly for thousands of centuries.

A resurgence of interest in acorns - and the Oak as a 'bread and butter tree' - occurred during the food shortages of the World Wars where it was 'rediscovered' that acorns could be added to flour to make nutritious 'acorn bread'. Acorns are easily prepared at home and provide high oil and starch content that is easily digested.

Nutritionally, these nuts of the Oak tree provided a very valuable source of food for early people. Arthur Haines writes:

> [The nut] contains starches, oils, some protein, the minerals calcium, phosphorus, and potassium, as well as several B complex vitamins (unfortunately, the B vitamins are water soluble and will

largely be lost in the final product). The protein is high quality protein due to its completeness.

François Couplan suggests bitter acorns contain 4% protein, 4% fats, 30-35% starch, 10% sugars, and 5-10% tannins and minerals.

Small amounts of tannins have an antioxidant effect. Tannic acid (tannin) is a water-soluble polyphenol that is present in tea, green tea, coffee, red wine, nuts, fruits and many plant foods.

Is it possible to eat acorn or acorn products without first leaching off the tannins and reducing the bitterness?

For myself, leaching is compulsory.

Too much tannin can impact your kidneys and liver. As the old adage says: "The dose makes the poison".

Personally I value my internal organs, so I spend quite a bit of time leeching out the tannin. You'll find instructions on how to do this under the 'Recipe' section.

There are reports of dried and milled acorn used in Estonia, on occasion, without special leaching processes to improve the flavour. This usage was rare.

Euell Gibbons in Stalking the wild asparagus recalls foraging for acorns from the different species of Oaks in North America, and found them "considerably improved" after roasting, although his experience convinced him that "even unleached acorns of some species are worth the attention of anyone who is really hungry".

Haines provides several forager-tips for collecting acorns, including allowing the first crop that fall from the trees in autumn to remain on the ground, "[they] are generally immature or damaged by some pathogen", and waiting for larger quantities to fall in the second crop later in the month.

Vigilance is also required against pests of acorns that ruin the nuts in many foragers' crops. To separate the wheat from the chaff, so to speak, observe the attached cup (which should detach easily if the acorn is not infected), finding exit holes of grubs, avoiding dull brown or grey acorns likely to be old nuts from the past season, finding darkened areas, dark spots or a rippled bottom on bad acorns, or noticing whether the shell has slipped away from the nut.

In other words, inspect your wild edibles as closely as you would fruit or vegetables selected from your vegetable patch, the supermarket or market - use your common sense.

Finally, a float test will determine whether an acorn is good or bad - simply put the acorns in a bowl of water and discard those that float to the top. Once the best acorns have been selected, it's good to prepare them quickly for eating, cooking or storage (such as by drying) as the raw nuts have a short shelf life.

Acorn kernels were sometimes leached by burying in ash or charcoal and watered to leach out the bitter tannins. This method was used by Native American Indian tribes to prepare acorns gathered from their own native Oak species. Among some tribes, ground acorns were placed in a hollow pocket of sand with water trickling through to release the bitterness. As a result, the acorn meal was sometimes eaten with sand and caused teeth to be 'sandpapered' down.

Alternatively, acorns can be boiled in several changes of water to reduce the bitterness, which is kinder to teeth. My colleague Francois Couplan suggests any bitterness that remains in the 'acorn mush' can be resolved by mixing with milk. The mush can be spread on a baking sheet and baked in the oven to make a hardened meal to be stored for months, or mixed with flour.

Anything that could be used to make flour was a valuable commodity for early people. Flour provided the means to make bread when other foods were scarce. Acorns could be dried and ground into flour and, once again, "with the flour first washed in hot water to remove the tannins and bitter flavour".

Acorn meal, despite being seen as a 'famine food', makes an excellent mix in flour for bread and cakes. My friend Toni Spencer (definitely an acorn Queen) makes all manner of delicious scrumminess from acorn flour. You are only limited by your imagination, and a bit of experimenting!

Acorn meal can also be added as a bulking agent to soups, stews and even burgers. The flour doesn't necessarily need to be reserved for 'famine bread' either, but could be added to recipes for cakes, muffins, waffles and other baked goods.

Acorns of different *Quercus spp.* have been used for food since prehistoric times and though many culinary uses can be attributed to different species, the uses are perhaps interchangeable between each one.

Some Native American Indian people have eaten acorns raw like chestnuts or candied the nuts like sweets. Canadian indigenous peoples resorted to various species of Oak for their fruits and leaves. The acorns were gathered from the ground in autumn by women and children for a variety of uses, such as snacking, roasting, boiling or drying into meal to add to other dishes.

Cooked acorns were sometimes mashed and eaten with animal grease or added to duck broth. A trend with American foragers is to use the cooked nuts for muffin batter or caramelised for candy. Similar uses can be applied to acorns gathered from Oak species in Britain, Ireland and Europe as well.

Not to say our own common Oak (*Q. robur*) has not been well employed as a wild edible. In Provence and Italy, acorns are mixed with dried figs to make a speciality bread. In Basque regions of Spain, it was common to eat acorns raw, roasted or ground into flour.

In Arab countries, a traditional dish called *racahout* is made from acorns, cocoa, honey, sugar or starch to 'fatten women'.

Children in Estonia snacked on acorns - raw or fire cooked - and ate Oak galls or licked the nectar from the leaves. Polish children also enjoyed raw or roasted acorns as a snack up until the early 20th century.

Finely-chopped acorns may be used as a substitute for almonds in most recipes, such as biscuits, flapjacks, baked goods and fish. Acorns also provide a source of a manna called *diarbekei* that is used in butter for cooking. It apparently tastes 'saccharine and agreeable'.

Roasted acorns have been used as a coffee substitute, being chopped and roasted, then ground up, chopped and roasted again, until they provide a suitable blend in countries such as Germany, Estonia, Poland, and the Czech Republic; in the latter, acorns have also provided a cocoa substitute.

In Germany, this is sometimes called '*eichel kaffee*' or acorn coffee. Acorn coffee was also recommended during the Second World War during food shortages.

From the nuts to the leaves and wood. Oak leaves can be used to make wine. In the Czech Republic, Oak leaves were an ingredient added to spirits. In Estonia, Oak was used to spice beer-like drinks and the bark was sometimes used for vodka flavouring. Oak wood staves for barrels were also used to impart an Oaky flavour, from the plant tannins, into beers, wines and spirits.

In the Baltics, Memal Oak barrels contribute vanilla-cognac flavour to wine, which is highly rated by the Coopers Guild of England.

In France, wine-flavoured Oak shavings from barrels may be used to smoke foods at barbecues. Similar uses occur in different Oak species, such as North America's white Oak (Q. alba) which is used in barrels to mature whisky.

Oak charcoal has been used to smoke fish for flavouring as well. Finally, an unusual use for Oak leaves in Estonia and Poland was as an additive to lactofermented cucumbers, which made the cucumbers dark.

If you can find no other use for Oak leaves in your kitchen, despite all these ideas, you can bake bread on Oak leaves to stop the bottoms from burning.

Amongst all these numerous and innovative uses for Oak as a wild edible, it's also recognised that species like our English Oak (Q. robur) was an emergency source of nutrition when times required it.

Even the trunk of the tree has provided an edible source of gum. In Poland, acorn meal was added to bread as famine food up until the 20th century or used to flavour bread. In the Czech Republic, the flowering buds of Oak were ground into flour during times of scarcity.

In Spain and Italy, around 20% of the food of poorer people once consisted of acorns. A French bishop of the 9th century had asked his priests to make sure his people had plenty of acorns during a food shortage. In Portugal and again in Majorca "roasted acorns are eaten exactly as one eats roasted chestnuts in America."

Across the globe the Oak provides diverse delicacies. The sawtooth Oak (*Q. acutissima*) provides *dotori muk* or acorn curd, which is eaten as a summer 'cooling' food with chilis, green onions and soy sauce. It's usually sold in Korean markets.

In Japan, the leaves of the daimyo Oak (*Q. dentata*) are wrapped around festive rice cakes called kashiwa mochi; *Q. aliena* acorns are also ground into flour for dumplings. The dead-wood of another species in Japan, *Q. glandulifera*, is used to grow the shiitake mushroom.

In south-west Asia, the acorns of the holm Oak (*Q. ilex*) are mixed with clay to make a cake or bread resembling soft chocolate or nougat. This delicacy is eaten with lard, milk, cheese or honey. In Mongolia, leaves of *Q. mongolica* are gathered to make a tea, brewed with Siberian crabapple fruit. In Tibet, the resin of *Q. lanata* is boiled in water to make tea.

The acorns of the white Oak (*Q. alba*) of North America are eaten oven-baked with butter and salt, or cooled as a salty 'nut' treat. The swamp white Oak (*Q. bicolor*) yields particularly large acorns in comparison to other Oak species. These can be ground into meal for bread and cakes or other baked goods. In California, the wood of the coast live Oak (*Q. agrifolia*) is preferred for smoking foods such as steaks and chicken in Santa Maria-style barbecues. The acorns were also ground into meal for bread and soups.

In eastern-north America, the Oak galls produced by gall wasps on species, such as the red, black and scarlet Oaks, were picked by children to suck out the sweet juice. The live Oak (*Q. virginiana*) is said to yield very sweet acorns from which an edible oil is obtained by crushing and boiling the nuts in water, then skimming off the oil from the surface.

For Native American Indian tribes, such as the Dakota, Iroquois, Ojibwa, Omaha, Pawnee, Ponca and Potawatomi, *Q. rubra* provided an important food source. The Italian Oak (*Q. cerris*) of Eurasia is harvested for a 'manna-like' substance called gaze, which is collected from the branches and boiled to reduce into syrup. The syrup may be mixed with flour to make a sweetmeat or used to sweeten other foods. It is also mixed with Oak leaves to make a type of cake. In parts of Spain, the acorns of cork Oak (*Q. suber*) are fed to pigs bred for gourmet pork products, such as chorizo, to give the meat a distinctive flavour.

Around 50 species of Oak are listed as a world economic plant with their acorns as a nutritious wild edible, suggesting the species is as important to us now as it once was to early people. Smith in his Tree Crops, published in 1929, asked whether the acorn had the wonderful quality of a factory food, while being easily and naturally preserved in storage. Could it be mixed with cereals or become a nut butter as popular as peanut? Then, of course, there is the tannin:

> How easy for the chemical engineer to get it out if he had 50,000 tons of acorns a year to deal with! Tannin is worth money. We scour the ends of the world for it. It is quite possible that income from tannin might put a premium price on bitter acorns.

He called for "Oak orchards" with their crops of acorn cereals to be grown on hills "now washing away as we plow them". Thus, the Oak is still a supreme wild edible worldwide in all its guises.

How to Dry and Store Acorns

Always gather your acorns green. This way the acorns are likely not to have been infested by larvae, beetles and rodents.

Take the acorn out of the cup and lay flat in single layers on a drying sheet, tabletop and allow to dry. They are ready when they sound like they have a bean inside them.

Store the dried acorns in their shell in large buckets with an airtight lid. The secret is to get them very dry and store them in their shells because the tannin is a natural preservative.

How to Process Acorns

Method #1

You can either process acorns fresh (green shell) or dried (brown shell).

First, you need to remove the nut from the shell. The easiest way is to split them in half using a knife. Then pop the nut out.

Discard any damaged nuts.

Put the nuts into a food processor with enough cold water to cover. Never use hot water at any stage when processing acorns. Then pulse until you get a mash, next pour the mixture into a large jar or bucket.

Place the jar under a tap (or use a hose) and allow the water to circulate and gently overspill for between 1-2- minutes.

Slowly stir the mixture. While doing this make sure the mash doesn't come out.

Pour off the water and refill one last time. Then cover the jar to prevent dust and insects entering.

Each day, pour off the dark tannin water and refill. Make sure you don't pour away the fine starch in the bottom of the jar or bucket. Refill with cold water.

Stir twice a day throughout the leaching process.

Acorns can take anything from 2 to 10 days to remove the tannin depending on what species of Oak used.

Once the leaching is complete. Spread the mash in layers no thicker than 1 cm on a baking tray. Then place in an oven at the lowest setting leaving the door slightly ajar.

Turn the mash every hour breaking up any clumps that have formed. Once dry (takes around 12 hours) cool before storing

in sealed jars.

Blend the mash until it becomes flour. The flour will store in sealed bags in the freezer for up to 2 years.

Method #2

Slice each acorn in half, and pop the nut out into a bucket. Fill with cold water and cover to keep dust and insects out. Stir twice a day.

Each day pour off the water and replace with fresh cold water. Repeat until the nuts taste sweet and you feel most of the tannin has been removed.

Acorns leached this way can take anything from 2 to 14 days to remove the tannin depending on what species of Oak used. Let your tastebuds tell you when they are done.

Once leached spread out the halved acorn nuts in single layers on sheets and dry in a low-temperature oven leaving the oven door slightly ajar. Takes around 12 hours, maybe longer. Or dry in a dehydrator.

When completely dry, place in halved acorns in an airtight sealed container and freeze for later use.

Spiced Pickled Acorns

- 550g whole/halved acorns
- 6tsp sea salt
- 500ml malt vinegar
- 150g sugar
- ½tsp ground black pepper
- ½tsp ground allspice
- ½tsp ground cloves
- ½tsp ground cinnamon
- 1tbsp freshly grated ginger

Cover acorns in salted water for 24 hours. Strain and allow to air dry for a few hours. In a pan add the black pepper, allspice, cloves, cinnamon, grated ginger and malt vinegar. Bring to boil then simmer for 10 minutes. Spoon acorns into jars, then cover with the spiced vinegar and seal.

If you get twitchy you can eat them after 14 days, but they are best if allowed to mature for between 3-6 months.

MEDICINE

As a magical tree, the Oak was believed to have the power to heal through all manner of peculiar rhymes and remedies, none of which impressed German mystic Hildegard of Bingen (1098-1179). She was rather scathing about the Oak:

> The Oak is cold, hard and bitter. It is a symbol of ruin. Oak wood and acorns are useless as medicine. Its fruit can also not be eaten by men; but some bent-backed animals such as swine feed themselves on them and become fat.

She didn't mention the sympathetic properties of the tree - for the Oak, like the ash, fell into a category of trees whereby a person could transfer their sickness to it and be cured. In the tradition of 'split-cure' trees, people crawled between a gap between two Oaks that had grown together, or used the bark as a 'nail tree' to stick their suffering to the Oak.

English diarist John Evelyn (1620-1706) recalled the belief that sleeping under an Oak tree "will cure paralysis, and recover those whom the malign influence of the Walnut-tree has smitten".

The mistletoe that grew on the Oak had many magical and medical uses. But that is the story of the mistletoe. Indeed, the Oak was thought to bestow magical healing properties to any other plants growing on its trunk or branches, such as the polypody fern.

English herbalist John Gerard wrote on the topic of Oak galls:

> ... that which growth on the bodies of olde Okes is preferred before the rest: in steede of this most do use that which is found under the Okes, which for all that is not to be termed Quercinum, or Polypodie of the Oke.

He recommended these galls be ground in white wine vinegar to treat skin problems or to yield a black hair dye. The tannic acid in Oak products was also said to produce a decoction for blackening hair.

All parts of the Oak - wood, bark, leaves, acorns and gallnuts (the latter being swollen balls caused by parasitic infection of the tree, usually formed by wasps) - were used in folk remedies since the Hippocratic Schools of medicine.

Many authors followed the words of Dioscorides (50 AD) who described the tree's astringent and dehydrating properties, and the binding and haemostatic (stopping the flow of blood) qualities of its bark.

Pliny the Elder (77 AD) also wrote about the leaves, 'berries' and bark of the Oak in decoctions as an all-round antidote. He crushed acorns mixed with salt and grease from a wagon axle to cure malignant scleroses.

Oak galls had an even wider range of use from treating mouth diseases, infected eyes and ears, toothache, stomach disorders, dysentery, rashes, abscesses, skin ailments and burns, swollen spleens and regulating menses.

Oak charcoal was crushed and mixed with honey to cure anthrax, although given Oak was a supreme tree in the days of the ancient Greeks and Romans, which no one dare harm, one wonders where all this Oak charcoal was made available from.

The classic uses of Oak developed further in the Middle Ages as herbalists made more use of the leaves, acorns and galls.

Flemish healer Rembert Dodoens (1517-1585), or Dodonaeus, wrote:

> Oak galls stop pain and are useful against bloody excrement or diarrhoea ... Gallnuts are also useful against the softening and swelling of the gums, any swelling of the tonsils and the throat, as well as sores in the mouth. Gallnuts also stem women's flow and make a dropped uterus return to its place...Gallnuts ... sOak in vinegar or water, will dye the hair black and eliminate proud flesh ... Ash of gallnuts mixed with vinegar and wine stops every kind of flow and bleeding.

On the Greek island of Chios, Oak galls in wine were used to treat diarrhoea.

English physician Nicholas Culpeper (1616-1654) described the bark, leaves and acorns in his Complete Herbal of 1653. Like Dodonaeus, he recommended the Oak as a 'binding' medicine that helps to stem bleeding and vomiting, and which "resists the poison of venomous creatures" as well as "the force of poisonous herbs and medicines".

He described the distilled water of Oak buds as a remedy for inflammation, pestilence, burning fevers, liver complaints and kidney stones. He also wrote: "The water that is found in the hollow places of old Oaks, is very effectual against any foul or spreading scabs."

Dutchman Abraham Munting (1626-1683) even praised the moss that grows on Oaks for "sOaked in beer, and laid between cloths on the breasts of a woman, will heal these if they are swollen".

Folk records describing the Oak as a medicinal plant - in absence of all magic - are still held in living memory for curing mild ailments such as diarrhoea or ringworm. Plant folklorist Roy Vickery reports: "Diarrhoea: grate a ripe acorn into warm milk and give to patient. [Taylor MSS, Woolverstone, Suffolk]."

Ground acorns in milk were another remedy for diarrhoea, grated acorns in white wine were said to cure a stitch, and roasted acorns with cinnamon were good for a rupture (perhaps meaning a hernia). Vickery also provides us with: "Ringworm: get six leaves of an Oak tree, boil them and drink the water in which they are boiled. [IFCSS MSS 800: 219, Co. Offaly]."

Further back in time, Greek physician Avicenna wrote that the Persians inhaled smoke from the burning wood of our English Oak (*Q. robur*) to relieve diarrhoea and to reduce pain.

The bark of the Oak was seen to be the most practical part of the tree in folk medicine, despite the Oak galls being widely praised. An infusion of the bark was used to treat rheumatism.

In the Scottish Highlands, Oak bark infusion was gargled for mouth diseases and sore throats; the twigs might also be used for toothbrushes.

In Ireland, the bark was used for ailments such as toothache, ulcers and as a treatment for hardening the feet in summertime. David Allen and Gabrielle Hatfield suggest Oak was used more in Irish folk medicine than British:

> Collected in spring from branches four to five years old, dried, chopped up and then boiled, this has been valued as a gargle for sore throats in Sligo and Tipperary, to counter diarrhoea in Meath and for adding to a hot bath for sore or excessively perspiring feet (Donegal, Meath, Kilkenny) or a sprained ankle (Offaly).

Other uses for Oak as a medicinal tree in Ireland included for neuralgia, ringworm and pin-worm.

In various folk remedies, not specifically Irish this time, the tannic acid in Oak materials were also recommended for sunburn, freckles and pimples, or for complaints such as eczema.

In Suffolk, England, acorns were mixed with beer and gin to cure ague (a shivering fever) or powdered acorns used to treat diarrhoea. In Wales, Oak bark mixed with the magic of Midsummer's Day (the piece of bark was rubbed on the left hand in silence) was thought to cure open sores.

Native American tribes have used different species of Oak in their folk remedies for generations, including *Q. alba*, *Q. lobata*, *Q. velutina*, and *Q. rubra*. The latter, for example, was eaten to treat acute diarrhoea by the Cherokee, Malecite, Micmac, Ojibwa and Potawatomi. A compound derived from the leaves of the swamp white Oak (*Q. bicolor*) was also smoked by the Iroquois tribe and exhaled through their noses to relieve catarrh.

It was the tannins in Oak that gave it the astringent and 'binding' properties so valued by early herbalists.

Today Oak may be recommended as an internal or external medicine for various disorders from wounds, ulcers, chilblains, piles, diarrhoea, dysentery, colitis and general stomach complaints to sore throats, mouth inflammations, tonsillitis, and nasal polyps.

The bark is said to be antiseptic and so useful as a gargle for ailments such as throat infections. The bark has also been used as a substitute to quinine to help treat a fever.

As a cream or ointment, or simply the powdered bark, Oak may be helpful for various inflammatory skin diseases such as eczema, bruises, ulcers, chilblains and increased sweating, as well as rashes, itchy skin or scaly skin. Try an Oak footbath for sweaty feet too. Thomas Bartram also recommends lint sOaked in Oak decoction for acute eye complaints.

James (Jim) Duke who was Frank Cook's mentor (Frank was a world-renowned botanical explorer and also my plant mentor), wrote in his Handbook of Medicinal Herbs on Oak's medical actions: anti-inflammatory (helpful for problem skin), antiperspirant (footbath for sweaty feet), antiviral (tackles sore throats), and antitumour - as well as anticarcinogenic.

He indicates the tree in herbalism for all the above uses, but also indicates certain types of cancer. Indeed, research has shown that the cork Oak (*Q. suber*) may have anticancer activity. However, it's advisable that you always check with your doctor before taking a herbal medicine to complement treatment for any serious condition or disease.

Oak is approved by the Commission E for coughs or bronchitis, diarrhoea, mouth inflammations and skin problems (inflammation), which are largely the uses for which it is prescribed in herbal medicine.

In subtle medicine concerned with maintaining physical and emotional health through the harmony of the body's energy, Oak is one of the Bach Flower Remedies. It is taken to "support brave and strong people who never give up the fight, in connection with their health or everyday affairs, but who do not know how or when to give up and who have difficulty acknowledging their weaknesses".

Looking at the medicinal uses of Oaks worldwide there are common themes, though it's worth noting: *Q. lanata* in Tibet is chosen for its bark (applied for sprains) and resin (applied externally for muscular aches and pains or taken internally as a powder for bloody dysentery). Manandhar writes, "A paste of cotyledon [the first leaves of a seedling] is applied to scorpion bites."

The astringent properties of Oak tannins are found in different species, including *Q. alba*, which is used by some Native American tribes as a bark decoction for stomach pains. Acorns are also considered astringent and the mould that sometimes forms on acorn meal has antibiotic properties, according to Couplan.

SAFETY NOTE

Conway warns the astringency of Oak may decrease the nutrients absorbed from our diet if taken in excess. He recommends taking Oak internally for complaints such as diarrhoea for no more than three to four days. Oak tannins may damage the mucous membranes of the digestive system.

Kuhnlein and Turner warn that high intakes of tannin, such as are found in Oak leaves and acorns, have been linked to some types of cancer. They suggest eating the foliage - bark, shoots and leaves - of Oak can be poisonous, and that acorns should be properly leached first.

Topical use may irritate people who suffer from eczema, despite being recommended for eczema in herbal medicine, and in cases of damaged skin.

While there are no known contraindications to taking Oak as a medicinal plant or wild edible in relation to drug or supplement interaction, for people with specific medical conditions, or during pregnancy and breastfeeding, this is not proof of its safety. Remember to consult your doctor.

ROWAN
Sorbus aucuparia

134

FAMILY

Rosaceae.

BOTANICAL DESCRIPTION

Height: small, ornamental tree growing up to 20 m. Leaves: pinnate leaves with pairs of leaflets are dark green on the upper side and bluish green on the underside with toothed margins; similar in appearance to ash trees. Flowers: scented umbels of white-petalled flowers with creamy anthers. Bark: smooth, shiny, greyish-bark; the bark is said to be particularly attractive in younger trees. Fruit: berrylike, scarlet fruit; turn from green to yellow to orange-red as they mature. Foliage: described as a small, shrubby tree with slender stem and branches.

FLOWERS

April to May.

STATUS

Perennial. Native.

HABITAT

Deciduous woodland, moor, mountain rocks, mountains, river banks, roadsides, rocks.

OVERVIEW

The Rowan species *Sorbus aucuparia*, also known as Mountain Ash, was believed by early people to be a quickening tree. It brought life-giving powers and protected mankind. Its flame-red berries drew the respect of the thunder god, connected the tree to lightning and fire, and provided a powerful source of healing and magic.

The name Rowan is thought to derive from the Norse word rune, meaning charm. In the language of flowers, Rowan also means prudence which seems appropriate given that it was employed as a precaution against all evil. The history of this small tree is woven into a rich store of countryside traditions, from cattle rites and festival fires to personal charms and magical household items.

While not related to the true ashes, *S. aucuparia* is often called Mountain Ash because of the resemblance of its leaves. Today it's largely cultivated as an ornamental tree in parks and gardens.

FOOD

There are few mentions of the Rowan in classical texts, but it was regarded as sacred by the Greeks. The tree could only be eaten as part of a ritual to respect the ancestors. In Poland, the berries were a forbidden fruit and it was believed to be a sin to fell the tree.

Birds, however, have no fear of eating Rowan berries, which they love. Birdcatchers once used the berries as bait to lure thrushes and other birds. The Latin name, aucuparia (meaning bird-catching), and the Dutch name, lijsterbes (meaning thrush-berry), referred to this ancient practice.

The raw berries have a bitter taste unless you know when to pick and how to prepare them. De Cleene and Lejeune write: "The berries are bitter, and must be sOaked in diluted vinegar for eight to twelve hours before use and then strained." The bitter, astringent taste is improved after frost, which helps make the fruit sweeter. Merritt Lyndon Fernald and Alfred Charles Kinsey write: "The unripe fruit is very austere and has an unpleasant flavour, but when thoroughly ripe and mellowed by frost it becomes palatable."

Rowan berries are used for wide-ranging food stuffs including jams, jellies, conserves, marmalades, vinegars, wines, spirits, confectionary, ketchups, pies and soups. A Rowan-berry syrup can be made by draining the juice and cooking with sugar or honey. Such treats have been made with the fruits of the Rowan tree, specifically S. aucuparia, from Europe to India.

Rowan jelly is a versatile ingredient in cooking. Richard Mabey describes it as "deliciously dark orange, with a sharp, marmaladish flavour", while others say the berries are "very juicy, sour and bitter", but tolerable as a jam or jelly. It may be used as a substitute to red currant jelly eaten with roast dinners or other meat dishes, such as venison or lamb.

Mrs Grieve recommends Rowan jelly with cold game or wild fowl. The distinct flavour of Rowan berries, which can be quite overpowering, is balanced with apples. (Although a gentle reminder here that Rowan and apple trees are mortal enemies, according to folklore, and must not be grown together.)

Dried Rowan berries can be ground to make a flour for bread – perfect for spreading Rowan jam or jelly – or mixed with cereal. This practice has been more common in Europe in times of scarcity. An old gypsy remedy involved ground-up, dried Rowan berries made into flour to bake "small cakes for unwell children". The leaves have also been picked as a 'famine food' in the past, but they contain a cyanogenic glucoside (cancer-causing agent). So you should be very hungry before even thinking of eating them.

Rowan berries can make pleasant drinks from a simple infusion to a lemonade with strained Rowan juice and copious amounts of sugar; the latter can also be taken as a cough syrup. The berries have been used as a coffee substitute, the leaves and flowers to adulterate tea.

In Germany, Rowan berries are used to make brandy, added to Dutch gin or make a type of vodka in northern parts. In Sweden, the berries were among those wild fruits gathered to flavour hard liquor. In Poland too the berries flavour a vodka called Jarzebiak. In Russia, Rowan berries are an ingredient for some vodkas. In Northern Europe, they were used to make cider and other strong spirits. In Wales, the berries were brewed for Rowanberry ale, although the traditional recipe is apparently lost.

In Ireland the berries were a significant wild fruit, says Peter Wyse Jackson, with remains found among the excavations of Viking settlements in Dublin dating back 1,000 years. He suggests their bitterness was balanced with honey. The berries have also been used to flavour alcoholic beverages, particularly mead.

In the commercial food and pharmaceutical industries Rowan berries are a natural source of sorbitol. It may be used as a sugar substitute for diabetics being half as sweet as sucrose.

The berries are also eaten for their nutritive value as well as their sharp taste. They contain vitamins A and C, and other substances like pectin, malic acid and tannins. In fact, a Rowan-berry jam could be considered a low-cost source of vitamin C to spread on your toast in the morning. Candied fruits of the Rowan tree contain 30–40 mg of vitamin C per 100g. The seeds of the berries yield a fatty oil, although this may be toxic.

In Estonia, almost all parts of the *S. aucuparia* tree have been used as a wild edible between the 18th–21st centuries, including the bark, twigs, buds, flowers, leaves, sap and fruit. Food stuffs include snacks, jams, syrups, vinegars, wines, salads, decoration, and as a bread ingredient called kvass, which is used to collect secretions from ants.

The berries were an ingredient in a popular fruit wine. The sap was once tapped from the Rowan tree, although this practice appears to have been rare. Whereas a tea is commonly made from the fruits and flowers. An unusual usage of the twigs is reported by Kalle and team (2016): "[the] twig was peeled and put into anthill, ants bit it and sour liquid was licked by children [sic]".

In Canada, various species of mountain ash were valued for their "tart, bitter fruits". The berries were eaten, though sparingly, by indigenous people, including the Algonquin, Cree, Ojibwa, Nlaka'-pamux, Lillooet, Halkomelem and other groups of British Columbia. The berries were sometimes buried for storage to be eaten at a later time in the year. Alternatively, they were used to marinate marmot or other meat, or to season salmon-head soup.

Rowan Berry Juice

- 14 grams of Rowan berries (frozen then defrosted)
- 500ml water

Put the Rowan berries into a saucepan and add the 500ml of water.

Bring to the boil, then using a potato masher crush the berries as much as possible. Reduce the heat and simmer for about 45 minutes with a lid on.

Mash the berries again, then strain overnight through muslin in a sieve or colander. You should now have approximately 400ml of liquid. Add water to make up 500ml.

Rowan Turkish Delight

- 1tsp butter
- 450g sugar
- 300ml of Rowan berry juice
- 1tsp lemon juice
- 25g gelatine
- ½tsp of vanilla essence
- 1tbsp of rose water
- 1tbsp pistachio nuts
- 1oz arrowroot or cornflour

Butter a 15cm square baking tin and set aside. Put the sugar, Rowan berry juice and lemon juice into a saucepan and bring to the boil. Continue boiling until the liquid becomes thicker so when you drop some into a bowl of cold water it forms a hard ball. Remove from the stove and let sit for 10 minutes. Dissolve the gelatine in a 120ml of hot boiled water, then add the vanilla essence, and mix very well with a wooden spoon. Now pour this into the Rowan liquid and mix thoroughly, then our half of it into the baking tin.

Sprinkle smashed up pistachios around the surface. Next stir the rosewater into the remainder of the Rowan liquid and mix well, then pour into the baking tin on top of the pistachios, and set aside to cool before placing overnight in the fridge. In the morning turn out the Rowan Turkish Delight, cut into cubes and roll each one in arrowroot powder or cornflour. Makes: 20-30 pieces.

Rowan and Bullace Jelly

- 500g Rowan berries (frozen 48 hours or longer, then defrosted)
- 500g bullace (frozen 48 hours or longer, then defrosted)

- 1 pint of medium cider
- 500g cane sugar

Put the Rowan berries and bullace in a jam pan along with the cider and slowly bring to the boil. Simmer for 60 minutes. Strain through a jelly bag over night or for at least 12 hours. This should yield approximately 1 pint of liquid. For every pint of liquid collected, add 500g of cane sugar.

Bring the liquid to the boil stirring occasionally until it has reached setting point. Setting point is when you can put a bit of the hot mixture on a cold plate, wait until it has cooled, then drag your finger through it. If the liquid does not fall back into a puddle but leaves a path through it then your jelly is ready to bottle.

Wash your jam jars in hot soapy water, then dry and sterilise in a fan assisted oven at 150°C for 10 minutes. Pour the bullace and Rowanberry jelly liquid into the hot jam jars and cap. Store in a dark cupboard. They should keep for at least a year. Enjoy. Makes: 3 jars

MEDICINE

In antiquity the Rowan was a famed remedy for stomach disorders and dysentery. We are told by Pliny the Elder (77 AD) it was an ingredient in oporice and a cheese called saprum, the latter being crushed in wine and mixed with salt and dried Rowan berries to prevent abdominal complaints.

The advice of the classical writers was still followed in the 15th to 16th centuries, although with some criticism by Flemish herbalist Rembert Dodoens (1517–1585), better known as Dodonaeus, and English herbalist Nicholas Culpeper (1616–1654), the latter observing Rowan berries were less effective than those of medlar trees. Culpeper wrote:

> ... when they are mellow, are fit to be taken to stay fluxes, scouring, and casting, yet less than medlars.

Nevertheless, he added, Rowan berries could be dried and taken internally or externally in decoction "to stay the bleeding of wounds, and of the mouth or nose". Medical writer John Pechey (1655–1716) wrote of Rowan:

> The berries yield an acid juice, which purges Water excellently well; and is very good for the scurvy. The Liquor which drops from the wounded Tree in the Spring, cures the Scurvy, and Diseases of the Spleen.

In Irish folk medicine, Rowan, specifically *S. aucuparia* was a treatment for diarrhoea and haemorrhoids – echoing the tree's use as a herb in the distant past – as well as for kidney problems, diabetes, arthritis and scurvy. In fact, many Rowan species were once used to treat scurvy and we now know that they contain high amounts of vitamin C.

Another traditional use in Ireland was as a remedy for worms – a few berries were taken before breakfast for a few days – and to cleanse the blood. The leaves were made into a poultice for sore eyes, taken as an infusion for rheumatism, or smoked and inhaled to treat asthma.

> [Ireland:] an infusion of the leaves is a popular remedy for rheumatism (an oz. to one pint); dose, one wineglassful. The leaves, when burned and inhaled are said to be useful in asthma. [Moloney, 1919]

In Ireland, the bark was also boiled for a cough syrup. In Irish veterinary folk medicine, animals were exposed to smoke from burning Rowan wood, although the medical purpose is not clear.

The berries were again eaten for scurvy in 17th-century Wales. Also in Wales, the inner bark was considered an aid to expel afterbirth.

In the English countryside Rowan was put to good use in a number of remedies for various ailments. The berries, prepared with apple, were taken for whooping cough in some parts. An account from Kent in 1991, reported by Vickery:

> My late parents came from Poland after the Second World War, and my mother occasionally used…herbal remedies… Frost-nipped Rowan berries (the frost removes the sourness) were infused in vodka and after six months or so this was used as a medicine for stomach ache.

In Aberdeenshire, Scotland, the Rowan tree – which part is not specified – was valued as a treatment for toothache in the 19th century. In Moray, a purge was made from the bark in the 18th century.

Around the world, Rowan trees have been employed in different folk medicine traditions. For example, the Native American Potawatomi tribe brewed a tea from the leaves to cure a cold.

In present-day herbal medicine, the leaves or fruit are still recommended as a haemostatic (to stem bleeding) or for digestive disorders. Rowan may be prescribed for wide-ranging conditions, including for diarrhoea, as a laxative, for haemorrhoids, for vaginal discharge, and to promote menstruation.

An infusion of the flowers or fruit can help to ease painful menstruation, constipation and kidney disorders. An infusion of the leaves may be used as an emetic (to expel intestinal worms).

Both the berries and the bark have astringent properties put to use in wide-ranging remedies from diarrhoea to sore throats and tonsillitis. In the case of the latter, either berries or bark are prepared as decoctions or tinctures and gargled. The leaves may also be used to treat coughs and bronchitis. All parts of the tree are astringent. Its antiseptic properties to make it a useful herbal remedy for colds, colic or pneumonia, diphtheria and croup.

While our ancestors may have appreciated the medical actions of Rowan based on its mythological associations, we now know that the tree does have antibacterial properties. Modern research has also shown that a preparation of Rowan fruits, which contain vitamins C and P, improved capillary function in patients suffering from cardiac disease.

Duke lists Rowan berry as a treatment for certain types of cancer, but it should be noted that the front-line treatment for any serious medical condition needs to be directed by your doctor. Do consult with a medical professional before taking a herbal medicine for a specific condition or illness, or in combination with prescribed drugs.

In homeopathy, a decoction of berries may treat peripneumonia in cattle. And as a cosmetic in humans, Rowan berries make a fruity face mask to restore youthful skin.

SAFETY NOTE

The berries if taken in excess may irritate the gastrointestinal system causing symptoms such as vomiting, excessive salivation and gastroenteritis. Jackson also warns that the berries can be toxic if taken in excess, and poisoning may occur in children or animals who eat too much of the berries or seeds.

Hatfield writes that the seeds are toxic and should be removed if the berries are used in cooking or medicine. Couplan adds that the seeds contain a cyanogenetic glucoside (cancer-causing compounds) which may support concerns about their toxicity. If further convincing was needed, Grieve writes: "It has been claimed that these seeds killed a child, apparently by prussic acid poisoning".

Few herbals indicate whether Rowan is safe or not to take during pregnancy and when breastfeeding, and in this case it may be best avoided.

SEA BUCKTHORN
Hippophae rhamnoides

FAMILY

Elaeagnaceae.

BOTANICAL DESCRIPTION

Height: around 1.9 m tall. Flowers: tiny green flowers. Leaves: narrow, lance-shaped, alternate leaves that are covered on both surfaces with silvery scales. Fruit: the berry has an unusual structure – an achene within a membranous ovary wall, enclosed within a fleshy receptacle. These succulent, orange fruits are densely clustered on short stalks.

FLOWERS

March to April.

STATUS

Perennial. Native.

HABITAT

Sea cliffs, dunes & dune slacks.

OVERVIEW

Sea Buckthorn is an ancient crop with modern virtues, say many researchers of ethnobotany.

Its Latin name Hippophae is from the Greek 'hippo', meaning 'horse', and 'phaos', meaning 'shine'. The plant was used in ancient

Greece as animal feed, particularly for horses because it was believed to make their coat shine.

Mrs Grieve tells us that Hippophae was instead derived from 'giving light to a horse', referring to the plant's alleged power to cure a horse of blindness, or 'shining underneath', referring to the silvery underside of the leaf.

Sea Buckthorn has been used for centuries in food and medicine and has attracted scientific attention in recent years for its nutritional qualities and its potential medical applications. It has gained popularity worldwide.

FOOD

The fruit is edible raw, and are aromatic but acidic, or sour tasting. Some describe it as a 'sharp, lemon taste'.

Picking the berries requires a patient hand as they are strongly attached to the thorny twigs and so filled with juice that they may burst.

The scent and acidic taste of the juice is said to be wonderful in salad dressings or fish dishes. The fresh juice can also be preserved in honey and drunk as a tonic, or used as a sweetener for herbal teas, or a base for preserves or liqueurs. The fruit can also be pickled.

The fruit, or juice of the fruit, can be added to mineral water, sweetened or unsweetened, and drunk as a refreshing lemonade. The dried fruit, or leaves, can be used to make tea.

There are many uses for these versatile berries from adding to ice creams and sorbets to making compote or fruit quark, or preserving in jelly, marmalade, syrups and sauces.

Sea Buckthorn jelly goes well with desserts containing white chocolate, mousse and bavaroise, or a jelly made from the fresh berry juice can be used as a glaze. The dried or ground fruit can also be sprinkled over barbecued meat.

In Europe and Asia, the berries are prepared and eaten as a jelly or sauce that can be used as a condiment to cold meats, game (especially venison) and cheese. In France, Sea Buckthorn syrup has been sold commercially, and the berries used to make a sauce to accompany meat and fish dishes. In the Hautes-Alpes, Sea Buckthorn jellies were once very popular and the juice was used in vinegar.

In the countries bordering the Gulf of Bothnia, between Finland's west coast and Sweden's east coast, the berries are made into a jelly and eaten with fish. In pre-industrial Sweden, the use of the sour fruits was said to be restricted to the fishermen of the north part of the Bothnian Bay, who used them in a sauce for fish.

In modern-day Sweden, the plant has had a surge of revival in popularity. A jam and juice made from Sea Buckthorn fruits can be bought from Uppsala's weekly market. In Siberia and Central Asia, tribes consumed the fruit with milk and cheese.

Rural communities of the Central Himalaya use Sea Buckthorn berries, boiled in sugar, to make a traditional chutney or jelly. The fruits are also eaten as snacks by children, who appear to relish the acidic taste. Children in England, as well as the Himalayas, also favoured these tart berries.

The Bhotiva tribe use the juice and fruit pulp as a substitute for tomato or curd in vegetable dishes during winter. The use of Sea Buckthorn has seen some small commercial success as a wild edible in this region. The juice being made into a local squash drink called Himamesh. It's believed that Sea Buckthorn could provide a boost to the local economy, based on the example of this cottage industry. The seeds also yield a nutrient-rich oil with economic potential.

The plant has been further capitalised in China where, in connection with the conservation of the Yellow River Region and with the support of the World Bank, Sea Buckthorn, known as shaji, has been extensively planted in the desert by The National Shaji Commission and Yellow River Regional Shaji Committee. The plant is harvested and used for carbonised drinks, tea bags and seed oil.

In a study done in 2007, the nutritive value of Sea Buckthorn was evaluated in plants growing in the Uttarakhand Himalaya. The fresh fruit berries and seeds were collected from Mana, Niti, Bhyundar, Gangotri and Yamunotri valleys of Garhwal Hills for determining the various biochemical constituents (such as fat, carbohydrate, starch, and protein) and mineral composition (such as nitrogen, phosphorus, sodium, potassium, iron, copper, zinc, and magnesium).

The study concluded that the fruits and seeds from the Gangotri valley "possess higher nutritive value in terms of fat, protein, carbohydrate, reducing sugars and lignins, and those from the Mana valley possess higher starch and acidity content".

Sea Buckthorn berries are one of the richest sources of vitamin C (780 mg/100 g). Thus, a teaspoonful would cover a daily requirement of vitamin C for an adult. In times past, the berries were collected as an emergency source of vitamin C. Today, the fruit are still used for making ascorbic acid-rich preparations (Sea Buckthorn juice).

Both the berries and seed oil contain 190 and 106 bioactive substances respectively. Indeed, the seed oil contains "vitamin K (about 109.8 to 230 mg/100 g) which promotes blood coagulation because of its catalytic role in forming prothrombin".

The fruit and seeds are also a good source of potassium, which "plays an important role in the ionic balance and helps in maintaining the tissue excitability of the human body". The seed oil is also rich in carotenoids, vitamin E, flavonoids, fatty acids, plant sterols, sugars and phenols.

The watery juice from the berries has also been found to contain fats, as well as the seeds. Suryakumar and Gupta write: "SBT berries have a unique composition, combining a cocktail of components usually only found separately."

The study by Dhyani and team (2007) was based on the premise that wild edible plants in the Himalayas have played a prominent role in food and medicine, and that most wild plants are a good source of nutrition being rich in proteins, vitamins and minerals. In particular, rural people depend heavily on wild plants for food and income, as well as the potential to utilise wild plants for the organic food and nutraceutical industries.

In the past decade, Sea Buckthorn has attracted special attention from researchers worldwide because of its many uses, but China, say the authors, is the only country to harness its full potential in food, medicine and cosmetics. A study by Christaki (2012) also suggested that the plant had many medicinal properties (including cardioprotective, antiatherogenic, antioxidant, anti-cancer, immunomodulatory, antibacterial, antiviral, wound healing and antiinflammatory) that were worthy of scientific research. Further, Christaki writes in a review of the plant:

> Hippophae berries contain high amounts of natural antioxidants resulting in one of the highest antioxidant activities, among the medicinal plants.

Suryakumar and Gupta emphasise the antioxidant activity of Sea Buckthorn, linking it to the plant's immune-boosting and anti-cancer properties. In several animal studies, the plant extracts demonstrated inhibiting effects on damaging free radicals in cells and aided recovery from oxidative stress in various diseases.

> SBT [Sea Buckthorn] has been extensively used in oriental traditional medicines for treatment of many inflammatory disorders. Hence from these observations, the antiinflammatory and immunomodulatory activities have been scientifically proved.

A more recent review of Sea Buckthorn's nutritive properties, carried out by Wani and team in 2016, reports that all parts of the plant contain bioactive substances, such as:

> Vitamins (A, C, E, riboflavin, folic acid, and K), carotenoids (α, β, δ-carotene, and lycopene), flavonoids, organic acids (malic acid and oxalic acid), sterols (ergosterol, stigmasterol, lanosterol, and amyrins) and some essential amino acids.

The berries also contain B vitamins and folic acid. As such an all-round source of vitamins and minerals, Sea Buckthorn could be considered a truly medicinal food, being tonic and a boost to the immune system.

How to Harvest Sea Buckthorn

Snip small branches laden with the fruit. Take home and place in a freezer. Once frozen the berries fall off quite easily.

Sea Buckthorn Syrup

To make a syrup, snap off 500g of frozen berries and bring them to a gentle boil in a saucepan, then strain through a clean tea towel in a sieve into a bowl, squeezing the last of the pulp to extract around

400ml of juice. For every 200ml juice add 100g of sugar and stir over a low heat for around 10 minutes. Then put the Sea Buckthorn syrup in a sterilised jar and store in a fridge.

Sea Buckthorn Curd

- 200ml Sea Buckthorn juice
- 2 tbsp lemon juice
- 4 eggs
- 300g caster sugar
- 120g unsalted butter

In a heavy saucepan melt the butter, then add the Sea Buckthorn and lemon juice, sugar and eggs. Cook over a medium heat whisking all the time until the mixture thickens. Cool and refrigerate.

MEDICINE

The plant has been domesticated and adopted for use in the traditional medicine of many cultures. Since ancient times, it has been used for "relieving cough, aiding digestion, invigorating blood circulation, and alleviating pain".

Sea Buckthorn has been used in China since the Tang Dynasty, more than 1,000 years ago.

> Many of its pharmacological effects have been recorded in classics such as Sibu Yidian from the Tang Dynasty and Jing Zhu Ben Cao from the Qing Dynasty. It was used as a medicinal plant in Tibet as early as 900 AD. The references to the medicinal use of SBT were found in the ancient Tibetan medicinal texts, including the RGyud Bzi (The Four Books of Pharmacopoeia) dated to the times of Tang Dynasty (618–907 AD).

The ancient Greek texts of Theophrastus and Dioscorides also speak of its use.

Sea Buckthorn has been used in Tibetan and Chinese traditional medicine for so long that it is commonly known as 'Chinese medicinal plant'. Further, in China, India and Pakistan, it is known as the 'wonder plant'. In traditional Chinese medicine, it was used to relieve pain, ease coughs, as an expectorant, to improve circulation, and as a digestive tonic. More recently, the plant was listed in the Pharmacopoeia of China in 1977.

The cardioprotective effects of the plant, which have only recently come to the attention of modern medicine, have been known in Tibetan medicine for thousands of years. The plant was also used to treat stomach ache in Tibet, as well as disorders of the lung, colds, coughs, fever, inflammation, abscesses, toxicity, tumours, constipation, and gynaecological disorders. Again, many of the uses of the plant are now the subject of scientific research. In Mongolia and the Middle East, the leaves, or leaf extract, has been used to treat colitis.

Rural communities of the Central Himalaya use Sea Buckthorn in medicine. For example, the Bhotiya tribe of Niti and Mana valley mix the juice with sugar and boil it for a few hours. The thick, dark brown cake produced is used as a remedy for colds, coughs and throat infections. The plant, known to the Bhotiya as 'amesh', is also used to make a tonic to treat cancer. One litre of juice from the mature fruit is mixed with 250 gm sugar, and two teaspoonfuls took before bedtime. People living at higher altitudes use the plant in veterinary medicine. The juice is used as a remedy for poisonous plants grazed by cattle, sheep and goats.

In India, a syrup has traditionally been used to treat pulmonary complaints and skin disorders.

In recent years, the medical properties of Sea Buckthorn (Hippophae rhamnoides) have been intensively researched. The plant contains a large number of antioxidant compounds with versatile activities such as effects on "atherosclerosis, anti-visceral obesity, platelet aggregation, inflammation, adverse stressful situations, and that of liver injury".

Suryakumar and Gupta (2011) reviewed the potential of Sea Buckthorn to treat oxidative damage in the liver and concluded: "SBT may be a hopeful drug for prevention and treatment of liver fibrosis, but further well-controlled clinical trials are required."

In particular, the berries, seeds and oil possess antiatherogenic, hypocholesterolemic, hypotensive, and anti-inflammatory properties that could be explored in pharmaceuticals to prevent or treat cardiovascular disease, such as high blood pressure. The plant flavonoids and fatty acids might also relieve the symptoms of diabetes.

A review of the general medical properties of the specific parts of the plant has revealed its versatility. The branches are used to treat colitis and enterocolitis in humans and animals in Mongolia. The leaves have been used as a compress to relieve rheumatoid arthritis in Middle Asia. The flowers have been used as a skin softener in Tajikistan. Oil extracted from Sea Buckthorn has also been used in skin therapy for burns, thanks to its anti-inflammatory properties, including sunburns, chemical burns, radiation burns and eczema.

In Russia, cosmonauts ate Sea Buckthorn berries and used a cream made from the berries to protect against cosmic rays. In the Ukraine, the oil extracted from the berries and seeds has been used to treat burns and leg ulcers.

Sea Buckthorn has also been investigated for its ability to protect humans at high altitudes from the effects of hypoxia. The leaf extract and seed oil provided "significant protection against hypobaric hypoxia-induced transvascular fluid leakage in the lungs and brain of rats", write Suryakumar and Gupta (2011). However, the authors also note that further study was needed.

General uses for the plant include as a pain killer, wound healer and metabolism regulator (the juice, syrup and oil of the fruit); as a treatment for eczema, lupus, erythematosus, chronic and slow-healing wounds, and an eye disease such as keratitis, trachoma, injuries or burns of eyelid, and conjunctivitis.

Yance cites a clinical trial in which Sea Buckthorn oil has helped in dry eye syndrome, showing significant improvements in eye moisture and reduction in eye irritation.

The high vitamin content in the fruit and seeds of the plant make it useful for poor concentration, exhaustion, susceptibility to colds, recovering from illness, and as an allround, immune-boosting, health tonic. The plant is also considered to lower cholesterol.

According to research carried out by Dhyani and team in 2007, the edible parts of Sea Buckthorn have been used in China in recent years as a medicine to treat wide-ranging conditions, including burns, gastric, skin radiations, cervical erosion and duodenal ulcers.

Other studies suggest that Sea Buckthorn oil can treat damaged mucous membranes of the gastrointestinal tract, which make it useful for treating mouth ulcers, gastric ulcers and stress ulcers. There is also interesting research on the overall beneficial effect of Sea Buckthorn on gastrointestinal digestive function, particularly in children and its effect on children's growth.

The role of Sea Buckthorn on antioxidation, the immune system and circulatory system has been analysed, indicating that it has the potential and has proved useful in the treatment of AIDS.

It [Sea Buckthorn] also showed inhibitory effect in an HIV infection in the cell culture and antimicrobial activity.

There is also scope for further research on the anti-cancer properties of some compounds of Sea Buckthorn. Certain chemicals in the plant may also help the body to recover from adverse stressful situations or stress that can slow down healing. This may be due to the plant's ability to normalise the functioning of the neuroendocrine system and restore hormonal-metabolic status in animals.

It is believed the flavonoids in the plant are largely responsible for its antioxidant and anti-cancer effects:

They protect cells from oxidative damage, consequent genetic mutation and ultimately cancer.

Other studies suggest that Sea Buckthorn oil may be helpful in recovery after chemotherapy.

The leaves have demonstrated antibacterial effects against *Bacillus cereus, Pseudomonas aeruginosa, Staphylococcus aureus* and *Enterococcus faecalis*. The seed oil has also exhibited anti-microbial activity against *Escherichia coli*.

The berries too have been shown to inhibit the growth of Gram-negative bacteria. The plant also has antiviral properties against influenza and the Herpes viruses.

SAFETY NOTE

Few studies have been conducted on the safety of Sea Buckthorn, but no study has yet deemed it unsafe for use in food or medicine. One researcher wrote:

Considering the fact that no significant changes have been observed in organ weight/body weight ratios, of any vital organ studied (except liver and kidney in 1 g/kg and 2 g/kg body weight doses, respectively) and biochemical and hematological parameters in different animal trials with a lethal dose for 50% reduction of population (LD50) of >10 g/kg when given orally, there is scope for further investigations regarding its safety in the daily diet as a protective medicine.

Lang warns not to eat the berries in large quantities as they can be purgative and have been used as a vermifuge (treatment for intestinal worms) in the past.

Karalliedde and Gawarammana warn to avoid Sea Buckthorn during pregnancy and when breastfeeding.

STRAWBERRY TREE
Arbutus unedo

FAMILY

Elaeagnaceae.

BOTANICAL DESCRIPTION

Height: up to 6–9 m. Leaves: leathery, serrated leaves; dark green above and pale green underneath. Flowers: white, bell-like, honey-scented flowers. Fruit: red, round, and warty strawberry-like fruit. Seeds ripen from October to December and fruit takes 12 months to ripen.

FLOWERS

October to December.

STATUS

Perennial. Native.

HABITAT

Urban streets, downs, scrub.

OVERVIEW

Have you heard of the Strawberry Tree? According to several sources, it is one of Ireland's rarest trees found mostly in south-western parts.

Its Irish name is caithne and evidence that the species was once widespread across the country is indicated in place names: for example, Ard na Caithne, meaning 'height of the arbutus' in

County Kerry, and Daire na Caithe, meaning 'Oakwood of the arbutus' in County Clare.

The Strawberry Tree (Arbutus unedo) is also commonly found in Europe and the Mediterranean. William Turner (15091568), English naturalist, wrote in 1548:

> Arbutus groweth in Italy, but hath leaves like the Quicken tree, a fruite lyke a strawberry, wherefore it may be called in English Strawberry Tree, or an arbute tree.

According to early Irish law, the Strawberry Tree was classified as Fodla fedo, which meant it was one of the Lower Divisions of the Wood. As such, it does appear to have been rather overlooked in folklore and folk medicine.

FOOD

The Strawberry Tree yields edible fruits that are high in vitamin C and other valuable nutrients. The fruit was largely eaten by poor people in the south-west of Ireland and it was known for producing a lethargic effect.

Jackson quotes a writer in 1764:

> From the tempting beauty of its form and colour, 'tis not a little mortifying to find its taste so insipid. However, I know of no danger of eating more than one or two at a time.

Thus, the advice appears to be 'eat in moderation', although the same writer commented that the lake people in Killarney, Ireland, ate plenty of strawberry-tree fruit "without any sensible ill effect".

The tree's Latin name unedo, means 'I eat one (only)', which suggests the unpalatable nature of the fruit has been recognised since antiquity. English herbalist John Gerard (1545–1612) wrote that the fruit tasted "somewhat harsh" and the flavour was "without any relish". He referred to the ancient Greek physician Dioscorides' observation that the berries hurt the stomach and caused a headache.

Modern-day herbal writers such as Niall Mac Coitir agree that Arbutus fruits have an insipid taste and may be indigestible to some. TK Lim describes the fruit as "mealy and sweetish, but not very aromatic" and "rarely eaten fresh".

That said, the fresh fruits have been eaten in parts of Italy, such as Sardinia, and in other countries of Europe as well. Not everyone is in agreement about its poor taste either. Piers Warren writes:

> It does have a somewhat gritty skin, but the fruit itself has the texture of a lush tropical fruit.

Perhaps the trick is knowing how and when to pick the fruits. Some authors suggest the plant is pleasant enough to eat if picked ripe or overripe.

There are records of strawberry-tree fruits being sold in Killarney, Ireland, in the 19th century, but fewer mentions of the fruit being eaten in south-west Ireland in more recent years.

Jams, jellies and marmalades made from strawberry-tree fruits are more popular in Europe. It has been suggested the fruits may have had some significance to local agricultural communities for making this type of produce. The purpose of home-made compotes and preserves was also a way of extending the fruit's availability to eat all year round.

Strawberry-tree berries contains around 20% sugars, although a French recipe suggests an equal ratio of sugar to fruit is needed to make a decent Arbutus jam. On the sunny Mediterranean island of Corsica, the fruits are boiled to make a traditional preserve. In İzmit, Turkey, the fruits are eaten fresh or cooked as jam.

If you are not a jam-maker then strawberry-tree fruit can be stirred into yoghurt or added to cereals. Other culinary uses across the Mediterranean region include as confectionary, or for pie and pastry fillings. According to some authors, the Strawberry Tree is one of the most important wild fruit species in Spain. The berries are eaten raw as a snack or taken home for dessert. The Spanish also obtain a sugar or sherbet from the fruit.

Others say strawberry-tree fruits are widely used in Portugal, Italy, Croatia, Bosnia-Herzegovina, Tunisia, Algeria and Morocco. In Morocco, *A. unedo* berries are used in cooking to enhance the flavour of a dish. In Latium, Italy, the cooked must, mosto cotto, is an ingredient in traditional sweets.

In Europe where the small tree is more common, the fruits are fermented for wine, spirits and liqueurs, and in some places a cider-like beverage. On the Dalmatian Coast, Croatia, strawberry-tree berries were added to rakija, a popular fruit brandy.

In Portugal, the fruits are made into a strong brandy called aguardente de medronho. In Liguria, Italy, the fruits make an alcoholic drink called vinetta. The addition of the fruit to these alcoholic beverages imparts an aromatic flavour.

In Sardinia, the Strawberry Tree is famous as the source of miele di corbezzolo, a rare chestnut-coloured honey with a peppery, minty flavour. In Sicily, beekeepers have prized the tree for its contribution to koumaromelo honey. A sugar or syrup is also derived from the fruit.

Studies suggest that A. unedo has promise as a commercial fruit tree dependent on the propagation of certain characteristics, such as selecting the size of the fruit. Sulusoglu and team (2011) wrote on this matter: 'It will be possible to obtain more productive trees and better fruit quality which will contribute to the economy'.

Molina and team (2011) wrote:

> Furthermore, cultivation [of the Strawberry Tree] could be considered to obtain greater yields and to promote new potential uses in the food industry.

Their study found that the Strawberry Tree has a considerable crop yield that is only currently made of use for small-scale local collection.

As well as sugars, the fruits of are high in dietary fibre, beneficial fatty acids, a source of vitamin C, K, E and calcium, with a low sodium content (Sánchez-Mata and Tardío, 2016).

In fact, strawberry-tree fruits contain an impressive 520 mg of vitamin C per 100 g on average (Doukani and Hadjer, 2015).

Looking at the nutritional value of the fruit in Algeria, reminds us that vitamin C is vital in diets for helping to prevent and fight diseases. Doukani and Hadjer concluded that strawberry-tree fruits have:

> A high nutritional quality because it provides important bioactive compounds in health protection namely polyphenols that are antioxidants, dietary fibers, vitamins and organic acids.

The strawberry-tree berries have a wide range of antioxidant components that make them a potential 'health promoting food'

(Lim, 2012). Other studies support this view of its nutritive value. Ruiz-Rodríguez et al. (2011) wrote:

> Strawberry-tree fruits can be considered a very good source of health promoting compounds as vitamin C and dietary fiber...They are also rich in total available carbohydrates, sugars, potassium... These results...may help to reinforce its consumption, as an alternative to the fruits available in the market or a source of bioactive compounds for dietary supplements or functional foods.

Strawberry-tree berries are also rich in carbohydrates and this warrants their use as a snack-food to stave off hunger (Barros et al., 2010). Although if you're not keen on the taste then you might not eat the berries unless you were extremely hungry. Despite complaints about its 'insipid' flavour, strawberry-tree berries have high levels of sucrose and fructose; the latter is the sweetest of all naturallyoccurring carbohydrates as well as providing a good source of energy. Thus, it seems strawberry-tree berry jam is worth spreading on toast for an energetic breakfast.

In fact, in a study of three wild fruits – strawberry-tree berries, Blackthorn and rose fruits – Barros and team (2010) found that the fruits of the Strawberry Tree were highest in carbohydrates, proteins, sugars and flavonoids. The authors suggest that eating these fruits in the past may not have made a significant contribution to people's diets, but did provide vitamins and essential fatty acids not present in daily meals like bread and potatoes.

Other species of Arbutus yield edible fruits that are usually eaten raw or cooked for preserves and confectionary, such as *A. andrachne* and *A. menziesii*.

A. andrachne fruits were said to be eaten during the so-called Golden Age of ancient Greece. *A. menziesii fruits* resemble Morello cherries, while the tree itself is the source of a rare, medium-coloured and candy-like honey. In the Canary Islands, *A. canariensis* is used to make a sweetmeat.

There is no doubt that the fruits are the most eaten part of the Strawberry Tree, although the leafy branches have been used as a preservative for olives in Spain.

Referring to its use in Ireland, Jackson writes:

> In 1828 Prince Hermann von Pückler-Muskau, a German prince visiting Killarney, Co. Kerry, wrote: 'A fresh caught salmon broiled on arbutus-sticks over the fire was an admirable specimen of Irish fare'.

Goats favour the young shoots of the tree for their winter food. Other species in the Arbutus genus have provided fodder for animals too.

Strawberry Tree Jam

- 500 g strawberry fruit
- 200 g brown sugar
- 25g fresh ginger (chopped)
- Zest and juice of one lemon

Wash the fruit, roughly chop and and put in a pan over a medium heat. Stir occasionally so they don't stick to the bottom of the pan and burn. If they are not juicy enough, add a tablespoon or two of water. Simmer for about 15 minutes. Sieve, then return the mixture to the heat and add in sugar, ginger and lemon zest. Turn up the heat until it starts bubbling and simmer for about 30 minutes or until it turns glossy. Pour into sterilised jars, seal and store in a dark place.

Strawberry Tree Vinegar

- 200g Strawberry Tree fruit
- 500ml cider vinegar
- 2 tbs of Bonraw coconut blossom sugar

Clean the Strawberry Tree fruits in a bowl of water. Drain and put into a blender along with the cider vinegar. Pour through a sieve and allow to drip. You might want to smoosh the mixture with a spoon as the fruits can be quite gritty. Blend the stained liquid with the coconut blossom sugar. Bottle and store in a dark place. Once opened, refrigerate.

MEDICINE

This pretty shrub-like tree caught the attention of classical writers. It is mentioned by Theophrastus (371–287 BC), Pliny the Elder (23–79 AD), and Dioscorides (40–90 AD). But by all accounts they did not appreciate its fruit.

The Flemish botanist Carolus Clusius (1526–1609) described a water that was extracted from the leaves and flowers of the tree in Portugal and used for eye diseases, plague or poisoning. The English medical writer John Pechey (16551716) recommended a decoction of the leaves and flowers as an antidote against the plague and poisons.

Home remedies handed down from generation to generation have employed the Strawberry Tree for a variety of uses. In Spain, Italy, Libya, and Tunisia, the leaves or roots were decocted to treat diarrhoea. The astringent action of the leaves and bark were also used in Libya to treat kidney diseases. In Portugal, traditional uses of the leaves included as a diuretic, urinary antiseptic, an astringent and for diarrhoea.

In Algeria and Cyprus, a strawberry-fruit liqueur was drunk to prevent diarrhoea. In Cyprus, the tree was thought to have aphrodisiac and sedative effects. The fruit pulp was prepared as a liqueur just for this purpose.

Present-day herbal texts promote the Strawberry Tree as an antiseptic and astringent medicinal herb. Its antiseptic properties might explain its use as a remedy for respiratory problems and for skin complaints, among other disorders. An extract of the tree has been found to exhibit antiinflammatory properties.

The antiseptic action of the leaves is employed in herbal medicine for urinary tract infections, such as cystitis and urethritis. The tree's astringency is also useful for conditions such as diarrhoea and dysentery. The Strawberry Tree has been indicated as a diuretic herb (increases urination) and as a laxative. Duke tells us it may be used as an antirheumatic herb as well.

A naturally-occurring compound in the bark called andromedotoxin may be used to treat diarrhoea. The bark also contains 45% tannin which is an astringent agent.

As an astringent herb, *A. unedo* makes an effective gargle for sore throats. Try an infusion of the leaves or bark.

A study by Tavares and team in 2010 found that the Strawberry Tree (*A. unedo*) has higher levels of antioxidant activity than blackberry and green tea. Fruits and vegetables that are high in antioxidant compounds, such as flavonoids and polyphenols, may prove promising in future cancer therapy (Tavares et al., 2010; Barros et al., 2010).

According to the authors, increasing certain fruits and vegetables in diets may help to prevent a range of chronic health disorders, including cancer and heart disease. They say:

> Strawberry Tree fruit has a high antioxidant capacity resulting from a range of antioxidants including phenolic compounds... vitamin C, vitamin E and carotenoids.

Other research groups also discovered a high level of antioxidant activity in the fruit. Barros and team (2009) found that strawberry-tree fruit contain major fatty acids, such as linoleic acid, which help to reduce blood cholesterol levels.

A further study by Fonseca and team in 2015 found that A. unedo berries are an excellent source of fatty acids, plant sterols and other valuable phytochemicals that have "future applications with nutritional, pharmacological or cosmetic purposes". A study by Mariotto and team (2008) showed a leaf extract had an inhibitory action on certain cancer cells.

Several sources report that the leaves and fruit may be helpful in preventative therapy to reduce high blood pressure and arterial disease (Quattrocchi, 2012). Studies also demonstrate the effects of a water-based extract of the tree on blood pressure (Barros et al., 2010). Further research on water extracts of *A. unedo* were found to reduce blood glucose levels in diabetic rats (Lim, 2012).

Recent investigations revealed both antiparasitic and antimicrobial activity in leaf and stem extracts of *A. unedo*. For example, an extract has been found to inhibit growth of the common fungal infection *Candida albicans* (Lim, 2012). Thus it appears there is much potential for future research and applications of the Strawberry Tree in pharmaceuticals.

In North Africa, another species of Arbutus, the *A. menziesii*, is valued for having similar medical actions, namely it is antiseptic, astringent, diuretic, laxative, antioxidant and also antibiotic. It is used for stomach complaints, ulcers, sore throats, colds, burns, wounds, and skin diseases (Quattrocchi, 2012).

SAFETY NOTE

It is advised that *A. unedo* should not be taken during pregnancy, or by people suffering from kidney disease, despite the herb being prescribed for kidney diseases in certain folk therapies (De Natale and Pollio, 2012)

With this in mind, it may be best avoided when breastfeeding as well.

It has been suggested that the Strawberry Tree could be intoxicating and narcotic (Duke, 2002).

SWEET CHESTNUT
Castanea sativa

FAMILY

Fagaceae.

BOTANICAL DESCRIPTION

Height: around 30m (98.4 ft). Branches and trunk: the trunk is spirally twisted with a smooth, greyish brown bark featuring upright cracks or splits. Leaves: shiny, short-petiolated leaves (10–30cm/4–11in long) are oblong or lanceshaped from a wedge- or heart-shaped base with finely pointed teeth and 15 to 20 parallel veins. They remain on trees till late autumn and turn a pale gold. Buds and flowers: the tree bears both male and female flowers, or catkins; the male flowers feature 10–20 stamens and are borne above, the yellow-green female flowers display at the base. Both male and female flowers appear as stiff insect-pollinated catkins (10–20c/1.5–4in long). Some say the catkins have a sickly fragrance reminiscent of semen. Fruit: shiny brown fruit (3.5cm/1.4in across) are enclosed by a two-to-four valve cupule featuring a spiky case and bristly tail.

FLOWERS

July.

STATUS

Perennial. Not native.

HABITAT

Deciduous woodland, hedgerows.

OVERVIEW

It is thought that the Sweet Chestnut was introduced to Europe from Persia around the fifth century and slowly became established. They have been cultivated in the Mediterranean region for almost 3,000 years. The generic name for the chestnut is castanea, which is derived from the town of Castanis in Thessaly where many chestnut trees grew.

From Turkey to Sardinia, and from there, the Sweet Chestnut tree spread through Europe. According to Peter Wyse Jackman, the Romans introduced the tree to Britain around 42 to 410 AD as a source of food for their legions, but the cool climate was not ideal for a good chestnut crop. The Romans had likely cultivated the tree by 37 BC, as described by Virgil in his Eclogues.

Miles Irving writes:

> "Chestnuts are one of the few wild foods that most people living in the British Isles have collected at some time or other, but most of this abundant food source still goes to waste. Every year a Chinese family congregates beneath a tree on a housing estate near me and fills carrier bags with chestnuts. They have it to themselves, yet there are enough people on that estate to harvest the crop many times over."

Richard Mabey warmly praises the custom of roasting chestnuts over a fire:

> "Chestnut roasting is an institution, rich with associations of smell, and of welcomingly hot coals in cold streets. To do it efficiently at home, slit the skins, and put the nuts in the hot ash of an open fire or close to the red coals – save one, which is put in uncut. When this explodes, the others are ready. The explosion is fairly fero-

cious, scattering hot shrapnel over the room, so sit well back from the fire and make sure all the other nuts have been slit."

Thus, the chestnut falls into that small group of wild edibles that most of us are familiar with and fond of.

Importantly, do not confuse Sweet Chestnuts with horse chestnuts. This notebook focuses on the customs and uses of the fruits, and leaves, flowers, buds, of the Sweet Chestnut tree (*Castanea sativa*), not the horse chestnut (*Aesculus hippocastanum*).

FOOD

For thousands of years, the Sweet Chestnut tree has provided a staple source of food in the mountainous areas of the Mediterranean where cereals would not grow well. Ancient Greeks and Romans, such as Dioscorides and Galen, provide testimony to the popularity of chestnuts by commenting on the flatulence caused by this diet. In Pliny's time, chestnuts were roasted and eaten by women who were fasting. Xenophon wrote that the children of the Persian nobility were fattened on chestnuts.

John Evelyn wrote of the good reputation of chestnuts as "delicacies for princes and a lusty and masculine food for rusticks, and able to make women well-complexioned". He also expressed his regret that chestnuts were not used as much as they should be in England:

> "But we give that fruit to our swine in England, which is amongst the delicacies of princes in other countries;...The best tables in France and Italy make them a service, eating them with salt, in wine or juice of lemmon and sugar; being first roasted in embers on the chaplet; and doubtless we might propagate their use

amongst our common people, being a food so cheap, and so lasting."

Abraham Munting's herbal in the seventeenth century reported: "Out of need, poor folk living in the mountains use these fruits [chestnuts] to make bread so as to be able to remain alive." Rembert Dodoens (Dodonaeus) herbal (1664) also records the practice of using Sweet Chestnut flour to make bread. The practice of Sweet Chestnut flour as a famine food has continued in the traditions of some countries. In Corsica, for example, people still serve a cooked Sweet Chestnut flour polenta and in parts of France, bread is still baked with Sweet Chestnut flour. Flour made from the seeds is still used in Mediterranean cooking, particularly in Italy.

By the nineteenth century, an Italian agronomist wrote on Tuscany that "the fruit of the chestnut tree is practically the sole subsistence of our highlanders". In the twentieth century, an Italian author mentioned that chestnuts were not only eaten as nuts but ground into flour for breadmaking. He was referring specifically to the 'wooden bread' eaten daily in Corsica. In fact, these plentiful nuts can be prepared in countless ways like wheat or potatoes. According to Corsican tradition, twenty two different dishes are made from chestnut flour for a wedding day feast.

In the southern Alps, people ate Sweet Chestnuts for centuries as part of their basic sustenance. In 1963, a community could own a slope for growing Sweet Chestnuts. De Cleene and Lejeune write: "This 'planting right' is called jus planti." Patience Gray in Honey From A Weed (2002) provides a charming account of a traditional Sweet Chestnut dessert that is eaten in the Apuanian Alps. Here, in the village of Castagnaccio, Spanish chestnut flour has provided a basic diet for centuries.

"Polenta was made of chestnut flour and castagnaccio, a kind of rustic torta which has the consistency of a pudding and the aspect of a shallow cake. It used to be made in round shallow copper and brass pans, which were set in the ashes of the fire. In the last war, chestnuts, fungi and weed were the only form of nourishment, unless the Castelpoggians undertook dangerous expeditions across the mountains, on foot, to Parma, a four day tramp often under fire, to barter their chestnut flour and salt for cheese and oil. Some people went on making this cake, baking it in the village bread oven, others preferred to forget it."

Gray adds that Castagnaccio is sold in winter in the Piazza delle Erbe in Verona from a stall also selling "winter pears, fritelle (fritters) and huge hot doughnuts cooked on the spot in boiling oil". James Duke also corroborates the stories of chestnut's uses as a staple food still in some areas of Europe: "In some European mountainous regions, chestnuts are still the staff of life, taking the place of wheat and potatoes in the form of chestnut flour, chestnut bread, and mashed chestnuts."

Italy is one of the biggest commercial growers of chestnuts, particularly the area around Parma according and exported wholesale. The chestnuts are made into confections, marrons glaces, and so on. De Cleene and Lejeune write: "Certain chestnut varieties are selected, which produce a particularly good yield: the Marron de Lyon is extremely well known because it bears fruit very early." A souffle of Sweet Chestnut is served as part of a main dish or as a dessert, and a puree made from the nuts can be served with game. In Italy, chestnuts that are dried for winter storage are called secchielli and in Spain pilongas. Dried chestnuts are sOaked or steamed before use.

In the Mediterranean to Corsica, Sweet Chestnut trees are grown mainly for the fruits (chestnuts), which are eaten roasted or boiled as Marrons. The nuts are also made into a flour called Farine de Chataignes, made into soup, a stuffing for poultry, fried in oil for Paltenta, Pattoni, and Nicoi, and used in confectionary for Marron Glace, used for brandy, to flavour beer (in France and Switzerland, and a local variety of beer in Corsica) and even as a coffee substitute. Sturtevant traces a traditional diet through the corridors of the Mediterranean:

> "Chestnuts afford a great part of the food of the peasants in the mountains of Madeira. In Sicily, chestnuts afford the poorer class of people their principal food in some parts of the isle; bread and puddings are made of the flour. In Tuscany, they are ground into flour and chiefly used in the form of porridge or pudding. In the coffeehouses of Lucca, Peseta and Pistoja, pates, muffins, tarts and other articles are made of chestnuts and are considered delicious. In Morea, chestnuts now form the principal food of the people for the whole year."

Chestnuts are a truly versatile nut, according to The Cambridge World History of Food: "Chestnuts also become jam and vanilla-chestnut cream, and they are candied. When dried, they can also be eaten raw, but they are usually ground into flour or made into a porridge, soup, or mash (polenta in Italy) and mixed with vegetables, meat, and lard. As flour, chestnuts become bread or pancakes and thickeners for stews." Chestnuts can be eaten raw, as a snack, or boiled as a vegetable, steamed, roasted, pureed, made into fritters, or dressed for meats and poultry.

James Duke writes: "In Italy, they are prepared like stew with gravy. Dried nuts used for cooking purposes as fresh nuts, or eaten like peanuts. Culled chestnuts used safely for fattening poultry and hogs. Cattle will also eat them. Used...for thickening soups, fried in oil; ...and as a source of oil." Chestnut is also a popular flavouring in the chocolate used for cakes and gateaux, and chestnut ice cream.

Mabey writes: "They can be pickled, candied, or made into an amber with breadcrumbs and egg yolk. Boiled with Brussels sprouts they were Goethe's favourite dish. Chopped, stewed and baked with red cabbage, they make a rich vegetable pudding."

Roasted chestnuts are traditionally sold on streets in mainland Europe and in Britain around Christmas time. Irving writes:

> "Chestnuts are traditional Christmas fare, but if you just keep them in a cupboard they will be dry and shrivelled by then. An old gypsy named Elijah taught me how to keep them fresh for longer by burying them in a big onion bag (or anything similar with plenty of holes). The dampness of the soil prevents the nuts from drying out so that they remain fresh and moist, although they will not last beyond Christmas without starting to sprout."

A sugar can also be extracted from the nuts. Indeed, according to The Cambridge World History of Food: "They [chestnuts] very nearly became the raw material for the production of sugar. Antoine Parmentier (that same great apothecary who granted the potato the dignity of human food) extracted sugar from the nuts and sent a chestnut sugarloaf weighing several pounds to the Academy in Lyon (Parmentier 1780). Research on the possibility of placing chestnuts at the center of the French sugar industry was intensified a few years later during the Continental blockade of the early nineteenth century. Napoleon's choice, however, was to make sugar from beets."

Nutritionally, chestnuts are rich in carbohydrates, high in protein (although their protein content is less than other nuts) and low in fat and cholesterol. Chestnut flour is valued for containing neither gluten or cholesterol, for example, as well as being low in fat, although they do contain a large amount of starch. Chestnuts are also unique among nuts in being high in vitamin C. Lim (2012) writes:

"Chestnut with a low fat content, completely free of cholesterol, a low sodium and high potassium content, moderate but high quality protein content, and rich in energy, vitamin C and amino acids especially lysine, tryptophan and sulphur containing amino acids provide a balanced and quality food. Chestnuts also contained folate and vitamin Bs and A and the macro minerals."

Lim adds that most chestnuts are consumed after processing which affects their nutritional value, although this is not all bad news:

"The cooking processes was found to significantly affect primary and secondary metabolite composition of chestnuts. Roasted chestnuts had higher protein contents, insoluble and total dietary fibre and lower fat contents whilst boiled chestnuts had lower protein, but higher fat contents. Cooking increased citric acid contents, especially in roasted chestnuts. In contrast, raw chestnuts had higher malic acid contents than cooked chestnuts. Moreover, roasted chestnuts had significantly higher gallic acid and total phenolic contents, and boiled chestnuts had higher gallic and ellagic acid contents, when compared to raw chestnuts. The data confirmed cooked chestnuts to be a good source of organic acids and phenolics and with low fat contents, properties that associated with positive health benefits."

Recognising that chestnuts are an important food source in many European countries, Vasconcelos and team (2010) reviewed the different health benefits that the fruit can provide largely based on the bioactive non-nutrients such as phenolics. The authors concluded that chestnuts can provide numerous health benefits for humans and animals in diet, but that to realise their true potential, improvements must be made in their production and processing, particularly at an industrial level.

> "From the various composition and health studies it is clear that chestnut fruits, and potentially other extracts from chestnut trees, have considerable potential as functional foods or as food ingredients, e.g. chestnut polyphenolic extracts as a natural source of antioxidants and other beneficial compounds such as gallic and ellagic acids and the ellagitannins."

Further, as chestnuts do not contain gluten and can be used to make flour for other products, the fruit may prove a useful and nutritious addition to the diet for people who suffer from Coeliac disease. Chestnut bread is said to be characterised by large, irregular holes, because it lacks gluten to bind the bread together and can only be used in moderate amounts. A higher amount of chestnut meal is used in Italian necci – flat cakes baked on hot stones and resembling Indian chapatti.

Sweet Chestnut leaves have been used to wrap certain cheeses, Banon, Dreux a la Feuille and Couhe Verac. Sweet Chestnut flowers yield a dark amber honey with a slightly bitter flavour that is valued in parts of France, and used in baking in Italy.

According to the Food and Agriculture Organization (FAO), worldwide chestnut production is estimated at about 1.1 million tons. Chestnut is an important food resource in several countries and is regaining interest in Europe.

Wild Winter Chestnut Soup

- 500g of Sweet Chestnuts

- 1 litre vegetable stock
- 3 bay leaves
- ½ tsp of vanilla powder
- Double goats cream

Slit the chestnuts and boil for 10 minutes. Then roast chestnuts at 200C for 15 minutes. Shell the chestnuts and return to pan with stock and 2 bay leaves and simmer for 5 minutes with the lid off. Next tear the remaining bay leaf to release the aromatic oils and add to the pan along with the vanilla powder and simmer for a further 5 minutes with the lid on. Finally blend and drizzle the double goats cream onto the served soup just before serving.

Chestnut Soufflé

Take 500g of Sweet Chestnuts, make a small slit in them and boil in salted water until soft. The timing will vary depending on their size. Peel them and place in a bowl and mash them up, you might want to add a little sugar, a sprinkling of sea salt and if too dry moisten with a little milk. Next mix in four beaten egg yolks. Then whip the four egg whites stiffly and slowly fold them into the chestnut mix. Butter a soufflé dish and pour the mixture into it and bake at 350°F, 180°C or 160° fan oven for twelve minutes. Serve immediately.

Chestnut Pate

Heat the oven to 425°F, 220°C or 200° fan, then take 500g of Sweet Chestnuts, make a cross in them in them, arrange on a baking tray and cook until the skin starts to peel back from the crosses. Put them in an old tea towel, wrap them up and squeeze hard until you hear the skins crackle. Let them sit for a couple of minutes then peel and put the flesh into a food processor. Add some raisins, the amount depends on your preference along with some soft butter or olive oil. Add powdered ginger, sea salt and black pepper. Pulse until smooth and everything is mixed in well, then adjust the seasoning according to your taste. Spoon into a storage tub and refrigerate overnight before using.

MEDICINE

Like many trees, Sweet Chestnut was used as a charm for healing. In Germany, for example, a chestnut was carried in pockets to protect against back pain, while in the US, a chestnut in the pocket was believed to protect against rheumatism.

In Waterland, the Netherlands, a chestnut (from the either the Sweet Chestnut or horse chestnut trees) or a piece of stolen potato, along with a piece of yellow sulphur, was carried as an amulet to ward off rheumatism.

In Flanders, Belgium, a chestnut (again, from either the sweet or horse chestnut trees) was carried to ward off rheumatism and gout; this custom was observed until recent times. Also in Belgium, in Limburg, a decoction of chestnut blossoms was used to rub parts of the body affected by gout.

In England, chestnuts were believed to have healing powers if they had been begged or borrowed. In gypsy traditions, chestnuts were worn in a bag around the neck to prevent piles. The bag must never be made of silk.

A classic tree ritual – Sweet Chestnuts were used as pin trees. In Bruges, where a Sweet Chestnut tree stood by a statute of the Virgin Mary, people stuck pins in the tree to ward off warts and ulcerations; this ritual was observed up until 1898.

The chestnut was discovered early on in medicine with records of its use by Dioscorides (c50 AD) and Pliny the Elder (77 AD). The latter recommended chestnuts for treating "vomiting, diarrhoea and haemoptysis, to stimulate peristalsis of the intestines and to increase the growth of flesh". Dioscorides and Galen both commented on the medicinal properties of chestnuts which were believed to protect against poisons, the bite of a mad dog, and dysentery. In the Middle Ages, raw chestnut seeds were used in the treatment of heart disorders.

These practices continued in Renaissance herbals, such as the herbals of the Fleming Rembert Dodoens (Dodonaeus) (1554) and the Englishman John Gerard (1597). Gerard wrote

"Our common Chestnuts are very dry and binding, and be nither hot nor cold, but in a mean betweene both: yet have they in them a certain windinesse, and by reason of this, unless the shell be firest cut, they skip suddenly with a cracke out of the fire whilest they be rosting...Being boiled or rosted they are not of so hard digestion. Some affirme, that of raw Chestnuts dried, and afterwards turned into meale, there is made a kinde of bread: yet it must needs be, that this should be dry and brittle, hardly concocted, and verie slow in passing thorow the belly."

Englishman Nicholas Culpeper's Complete Herbal (1653) states:

"The tree is abundantly under the dominion of Jupiter, and therefore the fruit must needs breed good blood, and yield commendable nourishment to the body; yet if eaten over-much, they make the blood thick, procure head ache, and bind the body; the inner skin, that covers the nut, is of so binding a quality, that a scruple of it being taken by a man, or ten grains by a child, soon stops any flux whatsoever. The whole nut being dried and beaten into powder, and a dram taken at a time, is a good remedy to stop the terms in women. If you dry Chestnuts, (only the kernels I mean) both the barks being taken away, beat them into powder, and make the powder up into a electuary with honey, so have you an admirable remedy for the cough and spitting of blood."

Dutchman Abraham Munting's herbal (1696) agreed with Culpeper's points.

Herbalist William Coles also accepted this medicinal use of chestnuts for under the Doctrine of Signatures, where the likeness of a disease was linked to its cure in the likeness of the plant. Coles wrote:

> "Everyone will be apt enough to discover the Signatures that this Nut beares...So that a small hint will be sufficient. It is not ordinarily delivered, that this Nut should stir up Venery...if the much nourishment they afford, and the windinesse going along with them (both which qualities are very conducible hereunto) be considered."

Although Coles also warns that the nuts can cause headaches and 'bind' the body if eating in excess.

These texts guided uses in early folk medicine where Sweet Chestnuts were largely believed to be good for the blood, as long as the nuts were not eaten in excess, otherwise the blood would then become too thick and cause headaches.

The leaves of Sweet Chestnut were boiled in water with honey and glycerine as a remedy for asthma and chest complaints. The tree was traditionally used in folk medicine for coughs, whooping cough and other respiratory illnesses such as bronchitis.

As recently as World War II, Sweet Chestnuts were still used in the home and kitchen for such remedies. Vickery writes of an account from Sussex where: "One lady asked them (them being my cousin and her charges, the school children) to collect Sweet Chestnut leaves, as she made a cough mixture from them".

Sweet Chestnut was also a traditional remedy for diarrhoea. In modern herbal medicine, Sweet Chestnut's bark, leaves, flowers and nuts are considered to be strengthening, calming, astringent, and digestive, even though the tree is not so well used today. Sweet Chestnut leaves may be used to treat diarrhoea, heavy menstrual bleeding and rheumatism, lower back pain, stiff joints and muscles, as well as occasionally coughs and bronchitis, and sore throats and pharyngitis (as a gargle), because of their mild decongestant qualities. The tree is anti-inflammatory, expectorant and demulcent. "The preparation tightens the mucous membranes and inhibits racking coughs."

In the Balkans, *C. sativa* has been used for swollen legs and painful veins. All parts of the Sweet Chestnut tree are rich in tannin, which make it highly astringent and thus supports these medicinal uses. For example, another use that traditionally indicates the Sweet Chestnut tree's astringent properties, is that the nuts, when crushed with vinegar and barley flour, can be used for inflammation of the breasts. As chestnuts are highly nutritious they are therefore helpful during convalescence.

Lim writes: "A hair shampoo can be made from infusing leaves and fruit husks." In the Bach Flower system Sweet Chestnut is taken: "extreme mental anguish, when everything has been tried and there is no light left".

Chestnut honey has antibacterial activity and has been used for dressing chronic wounds, burns or skin ulcers.

In modern research, Basile and team (2000) found that *Castanea sativa* has antibacterial effects against seven strains of bacteria. The authors concluded: "These results suggest that *C. sativa* is a source of bioactive substances endowed with interesting biological activities."

The antioxidant potential of *C. sativa* leaf was explored by Calliste and team in 2005. The study found that *C. sativa* leaf has antioxidant activity equal to quercetin and vitamin E. Antioxidant-containing plants are valued for their contribution to a healthy diet or to medicine, either home medicine or for pharmaceutical concerns, because of their preventative effects on free radicals – substances that ravage cells. Antioxidants can help to protect cells from free radical effects and thus also decrease the incidences of chronic diseases such as heart disease or diabetes.

Živković and team in 2010 looked at the antimicrobial, and antioxidant activity of Sweet Chestnut tree extracts, finding that the catkins, leaves, barks and spiny burs demonstrated the highest antimicrobial activity. The authors also found that there was: "Very significant and significant correlations were established between the antimicrobial activity of extracts and O2 radicals scavenging in all samples examined. The extracts of *Castanea sativa* are important sources of components active in reducing the level of oxidative stress." Chiarini and team (2013) found that Sweet Chestnut bark had high antioxidant activity that might have a cardioprotective effect.

A study by Carocho and team in 2014 partially corroborated the historical claims of the health benefits of Sweet Chestnut flowers, although ultimately concluded that more research is needed. The study found that extracts of the flowers contained a high quantity of flavonoids and exhibited high antioxidant activity. "Pharmaceutical industries could use the flowers as excipients for dietary supplements, benefiting from their natural content in polyphenols for health purposes. The food industry can use the high antioxidant power and natural high abundance of tannins in the flowers to preserve food and inhibit lipid deterioration and microorganism development." Carocho and team (2014) also explored the antitumor and antimicrobial effects of the flowers, again finding that ancestral claims were partly supported. "The antitumor activity, and lack of toxicity toward normal cells reassures the safety of consumption while the antimicrobial activity confers some applicability of these flowers in the food processing chain to be used as natural antimicrobials." Lim (2012) also cites a large number of studies supporting the antioxidant, antibacterial and anti-tumour effects of chestnut extracts.

In paediatric medicine, the seeds of *C. sativa* have been reported in the treatment of gastroenteritis and as a gluten-free diet in cases of coeliac disease.

SAFETY NOTE

People who suffer diabetes should not use Sweet Chestnut tree in food or medicine. The tannic acids in Sweet Chestnut tree may also ruin iron kitchenware.

Neves (2018) investigated the toxic effects of *C. sativa* where an infusion or decoction of the leaves are traditionally used in Portugal to treat cough in children, diarrhoea, infertility and hypertension. The investigation revealed that *C. sativa* extract may be mildly toxic and thus should be used with caution in children.

It would be wise not to confuse the fruits of the Sweet Chestnut tree (*Castanea sativa*), which are edible, with the fruits of the horse chestnut tree (*Aesculus hippocastanum*), which are inedible.

WILD SERVICE TREE
Sorbus torminalis

FAMILY

Rosaceae.

BOTANICAL DESCRIPTION

Height and girth: 20 m high and 15 m wide. Flowers: the flowers have five white petals and appear in branched clusters. Leaves: dark green with three to five pairs of toothed, pointed lobes; the lowest pair are deeper and wider, like the maple. Fruit: small, apple- or pear-shaped berries. Bark: dark brown to pale grey.

FLOWERS

Late April to June.

STATUS

Perennial. Native.

HABITAT

Deciduous woodland, hedgerows, scrub.

OVERVIEW

The Wild Service Tree is said to have earned its name from the Latin cervisia, because its small acidic fruit were used in ancient times to make a fermented, beer-like liquor. The name service-tree derives from the Latin word for beer, cerevisia because the Romans used the fruit of the related true-service tree (*Sorbus domestica*) to flavour beer.

The tree is also known as the chequer tree, which once referenced the traditional name for a pub, 'Chequers', when the chequerboard was a symbol for an inn or tavern in Roman times. The berries being used extensively for brewing.

As a native British species, the Wild Service Tree is now quite rare and its presence is often thought to be an indicator of ancient woodlands. The species, *Sorbus torminalis*, is now scattered in woods on clay and limestone soils throughout England and Wales; it is found most frequently in the Midlands and south-east England. While the tree is sometimes referred to as 'Sorbo', it has had many local names, so the berries are sometimes called 'Corniolo'.

In John Evelyn's Sylva, or A Discourse of Forest-Trees and the Propagation of Timber (1664), the Wild Service Tree is referred to as the chequer tree from Choker or the chokepear, which RCA Prior tells us, in On the Popular Names of British Plants, is "an antique pronunciation of the word which we find in the humorous old ballad of The Frere and the Boy...'Whan my fader gyveth me mete, She wolde theron that I were cheke'...i.e. chOaked".

FOOD

Vaughan and Geissler write, in The New Oxford Book of Food Plants, that such fruit from trees of the Rosacea family may be "of some local interest but of no great commercial importance". This statement may be rather sweeping, although it is true that the fruit of the Wild Service Tree are not widely used today, in the past it was a different story.

Gerard made little mention of the fruit except in medicine, but expressed a poor opinion of them as food suggesting that they should not be eaten. However, his warning was ignored. In Henry Phillips, Pomarium Brittanicum (1820), he writes:

> The fruit of the tree partakes of the quality of the Medlar, both in green and in ripe state. It is gathered in bunches and put into or hung on a cleft stick of about a yard long which becomes a mass of berries. In this state the fruit is sold by the country people and then hung up in a garden to receive the damp air of night which causes it to undergo a kind of putrefactive fermentation and in this soft state it is eaten and has a more agreeable acid than Medlar.

Indeed, the common consensus seems to be that the berries are perfectly edible after a period of 'bletting' in autumn frosts to make them turn soft and sweet. As a native tree of Britain's ancient woodlands, the Wild Service Tree berries are likely to have been eaten as long as humans have inhabited these isles. The fruit has been collected under various local names including sarvies, sorbus, service or chequer berries.

The fruit of Sorbus species, generally, including *S. torminalis*, are also an important source of vitamin C. The berries may be eaten fresh, or raw, after the first autumn frost, when overripe, or made into jams, jellies, syrups, conserves, vinegars and wines.

In the Elsass, or Alsace, a historical region in northeastern France on the Rhine River plain, the fruit are made into wine and brandy called Alizier-geist. Gray suggests that these sharp and acid-tasting wild berries are made more edible, even after first frost, by macerating in wine vinegar and sugar. In Salento, in the Italian peninsula, the fruit of service trees were once prepared by greengrocers and sold in shops till autumn.

Similarly, berries of the true service tree (*S. domestica*) also taste softer and milder, and are best eaten after the first frost. There is not much difference in usage between the two types of fruit, with true service berries also being favoured for making wine. Miles Irving says that the fruits of the true service tree have been used to make a cider-like drink on the continent, and that in Italy, true service berries have been eaten whole or made into jam.

In Medieval England and Wales, when the Wild Service Tree was widespread in lowland woods, the berries were used in jams, preserves and liqueurs. In the 19th century, the fruits were sold as 'chequers', as the tree was commonly known in the Weald of Kent.

The practice of 'bletting' the berries to sell at London markets and other shops in England has continued until fairly recently. In Sussex and the Isle of Wight, the fruit were tied up in bunches and sold in shops, mainly to children, as late as the mid 1800s. Children once ate service-tree berries as enthusiastically as sweets.

The fruit of *Sorbus torminalis* are described as small, greenish, and apple or pear shaped with dark spots, and an acid flavour which is made more agreeable and 'mealy' once exposed to frost. Once ripe, the fruit is brown with a chequered or speckled appearance, perhaps also alluding to the tree's other common name. The flavour of the fruit has been described as prune-like once fully ripened with a darkened cuticle, and having become soft and pulpy.

Mabey describes them like this:

> "The taste is unlike anything else which grows wild in this country, with hints of damson, prune, apricot, sultana and tamarind."

Ian Burrows who I met and interviewed only a few months before his death described the taste as like plum brandy "with strong overtones of dried apricots and sherry", adding that the fruit is "excellent raw or cooked". Taste is in the mouth of the beholder, and some have described it as sweet and sticky with the taste, and a texture, of tamarind and raisins. In contrast, the fruits of the true service tree (*S. domestica*), the related, non-native species, are small and green-flushed with brownish red, with many dots and lenticels. The taste is mild. In Worcestershire, true service berries go by the name of 'Whitty pear'.

The remains of service tree fruit have been found at prehistoric sites – the naturally sweet berries must have provided an excellent 'sugar' before other sources were available. If stored or preserved correctly, service-tree berries could be used through winter.

In 1992, Lisa Moffet published a study that looked at the organic material preserved in a post-Medieval latrine, which produced evidence for a wide range of cultivated plants. These included fruits, nuts, herbs and "at least one species of garden flower", as well as wild plants. *Sorbus torminalis* was included on the list of plants found in the latrine at Dudley Castle, in Dudley, northwest of Birmingham, in the north of England. The remains of the Wild Service Tree at the latrine suggest that it was more widely used in the past as a source of food than it is today.

In the Weald of Kent, in the south of England, service tree berries were a popular dessert fruit up until the beginning of the twentieth century. Gerard wrote that the Wild Service Tree grew in abundance in Kent. Richard Mabey also tells us: "The fruits were gathered before they had bletted and strung up in clusters around a stick, which was hung up indoors, often by the hearth. They were picked off and eaten as they ripened, like sweets."

A chequerberry beer was also produced by the Chequers Inn at Smarden, Kent: "'Pick off in bunches in October. Hang on a string like onions (look like swarm of bees). Hang till ripe. Cut off close to berries. Put them in stone or glass jars. Put sugar on - 1 lb to 5 lb of berries. Shake up well. Keep airtight until juice comes to the top.

The longer kept the better. Can add brandy. Drink. Then eat berries!'".

Irving quotes a major authority on the Wild Service Tree, Patrick Roper, who wrote in his Chequer: Wild Service Tree, that the berries were once eaten with "bread and potatoes, in brain and wild-service berry omelette, and in stews". The berries can also be "steeped in sugar and spirits to become the liqueur or cordial known as ratafia".

Around Europe, the Wild Service Tree has been used in local and traditional foods. In Bulgaria, the fruits of the Wild Service Tree are picked and stored for winter as a fruit pickle in vinegar or brine. In northern Dalmatia, Croatia, the fruits are gathered and eaten as wild edibles by villagers of the Lake Vrana Nature Park.

The fruit may be used as a base for beverages; as mentioned, the Wild Service Tree fruit are used for beverages including liqueurs and cider or beer like drinks. Alcoholic drinks, such as brandy or vodka, may be made from or flavoured by Rowanberry juice or fruits because "biochemical compounds that help to clear and preserve alcoholic drinks, adding flavour, astringency, bitterness, and extra sugars". In France, the service tree or Sorb-tree is known as Sorbier or Cormier. The fruits are harvested to produce a cider-like drink, as they are in Italy.

An ethnobotanical study of wild food plants in the White Carpathians in the Czech Republic (Pawera and team, 2017) interviewed 60 people from 25 villages and recorded the usage of 78 species of wild plants, including Sorbus species, which were listed as a culturally significant plant. Sorbus fruits are traditionally picked for syrups, jams, marmalades and brandies, or the leaves for tea.

The seeds of the Wild Service Tree are also edible. "It is soft and quite nutty, with a subtle almondy flavour."

Wild Service Berry Pie

- 4 cups of soft wild service berries
- ¾ cup of sugar
- 1 teaspoon of ground cinnamon
- 2 tablespoons of flour
- 1 tablespoon of lemon juice
- Ready made short crust pasty

Mix together the fruit, sugar, cinnamon and lemon juice. Pour the mixture into a 9 inch pastry pie shell and cover with a top crust. Pinch the edges together and bake in an oven at 375°F/190°C/170°C fan-assisted/gas mark 5 for 1 hour.

Wild Service Berry Vodka

- 500g of soft wild service berries
- 40% proof vodka
- 2 tablespoons of clear honey.

Mash the ripe wild service berries in a non-metallic bowl. Place the bowl in a warm place and let the mash ferment for a week or so. When ready pour the mixture into a jelly bag and allow to drip overnight, in the morning squeeze out as much juice as possible. Mix 1:1 ratio of juice to vodka and bottle.

Put the squeezed mash back into a bowl and pour ¼ of a litre of vodka over it. Mix well and allow to sit for two weeks before straining. Mix the original 1:1 mixture with this second blend, add 2 tablespoons of honey, mix well and bottle. Keep for a year before drinking.

Wild Service Berry Ale

- 4.5 litres of water
- 4 cups of ripe wild service berries
- 500 grams of malt dry yeast

Blend together the berries with 1 litre of water. In a large saucepan add the blended mixture together with the remaining water. Bring to a gentle boil and simmer for an hour. Take off the heat and allow to cool enough that you can dip your finger in without scalding it. Strain and press the mixture through a metal sieve. Add the malt extract and 1.5 grams of dry yeast per litre of liquid. Pour into a demijohn with an airlock. Ferment until the fermentation has stopped. Bottle and cap. Allow to sit for 6 months before drinking.

MEDICINE

The 17th-century English botanist John Gerard (1545–1612) wrote that Wild Service Tree berries were "cold and binding, and much more when they be hard, than when they are mild and soft". He recommended the fruit be used to treat stomach disorders, 'bloody fluxes', vomiting and to staunch bleeding – the latter, that is, if they are cut and dried in the sun before ripening.

Geoffrey Grigson mentions the griping quality of Wild Service Tree berries to fix matters of colic and a troublesome stomach. Evelyn also recommended the fruit for 'gripe', and, rather specifically, water distilled from the flower stalks for consumption and 'green-sickness' in virgins, and earache.

In Turkey, the boiled leaves were eaten to remedy diabetes or a stomach ache. In Northern Greece, Rowanberry fruits, in general speaking of trees from the Rosaceae family, have been traditionally eaten for both nutritious and medicinal properties, including as a remedy for diabetes.

A study by Gonciarz and team in 2013 analysed the antioxidant properties of fruits of forest trees and shrub fruits, including the Wild Service Tree (*Sorbus torminalis*), which are largely attractive to forest birds. While the smallest amount of phenolic compounds among the selected forest plants was found in *Sorbus torminalis*, the fruit of the Wild Service Tree still has "high antioxidant potential" and, say the authors, are "recommended for people exposed to long term oxidative stress, as civilisation diseases prevention". The authors also suggest that the fruits of these plants protect the wild animals that eat them, especially birds, against damages caused by oxidative stress.

Similarly in 2009, Serteser and team (2009) studied the antioxidant activity of wild fruits specifically in plants in the Afyonkarahisar province of Turkey. Fruit from various species, including *Sorbus torminalis*, were collected in spring. While *S. torminalis* demonstrated inhibitory effects against free radicals, its antioxidant activity was among the lowest of the fruits evaluated. The authors also noted that Sorbus species had lower iron-chelating activities than other fruits. "Chelating agents may have a great importance for rancidity of oily foods, even if they are not antioxidant materials. Because iron catalyzes this reaction during lipid peroxidation".

Nevertheless, the Wild Service Tree has been the subject of several studies to test the antioxidant properties of its fruit as the search continues for natural and safe sources of antioxidants. Antioxidants are substances that neutralise the oxidising effects of free radicals that ravage cells. In plants, many compounds are potential antioxidants such as flavonoids, tannins and lignins (which are all phenols) or other compounds which are grouped under tocopherols.

Oxidative stress has been linked to many diseases, such as Alzheimer's disease, as well as non-communicative, lifestyle-related illnesses. Hasbal and team (2014) researched the antioxidant properties of Wild Service Tree fruits, as well as the fruit's ability to inhibit acetylcholinesterase (AChE). "Inhibition of AChE serves as a strategy for the treatment of neurodegenerative disorders such as Alzheimer's disease," write the authors. "Alzheimer's disease is associated with aging and characterized by progressive memory loss and cognitive deterioration."

The authors also point to oxidative stress as a factor: "The brains of patients with Alzheimer's disease show a significant extent of oxidative damage associated with a marked accumulation of amyloid-b peptide. Some studies suggest that dietary supplements with antioxidants and free radical scavengers such as vitamin E may display some benefits in slowing the mild cognitive impairment of Alzheimer's disease."

In Hasbal and team's study, the fruits of the Wild Service Tree showed sufficient antioxidant and AChE inhibitory activity, although further research is needed to determine whether or not the fruit extracts could be used as a supplement in the treatment of Alzheimer's disease.

Mikulic-Petkovsek and team (2017) evaluated the antioxidant activity of nine types of Sorbus trees and identified Sorbus fruits as an important natural source of phenolic compounds. The authors also noted the link between high phenolic content and antioxidant activity, writing: "Due to their high capacity to scavenge free radicals, phenolic compounds are reported to have antioxidant and multiple biological effects".

Further, this antioxidant activity has potential to prevent food degradation and human diseases. The authors cite the traditional medical use of Rowanberry fruits in the management of diseases, such as intestinal obstructions, chronic diarrhoea, heart disease, cancers, diabetes and long-term diabetic complications, and inflammatory conditions. The authors also write that Rowanberry fruit have liver protective properties, "these fruits reduce hepatic lipid peroxidation by decreasing the bioavailability of alcohol and its oxidative metabolites (Lee and others 2006)".

The study concluded that "Since flavonoids represent potent antioxidant agents and have positive effects on human health, Sorbus fruit products could be recommended as valuable resource of these compounds"; and that "Additionally, it is important to highlight that Sorbus plants are easy to cultivate and are appropriate for areas with lower temperatures and miserable soil environments".

However, *Sorbus torminalis* did demonstrate the lowest phenolic content and thus antioxidant activity of all Rowanberry fruits evaluated in this particular study.

The unique chemistry of phenolic compounds in a plant species has been found to have a link to the antioxidant activity of the plant material, according to a study by Olszewska (2009). The author attributed the high levels of phenolic compounds to the biological activities of Sorbus species. While the study again proved that the antioxidant capacities of S. torminalis were lower than in other Sorbus species, the author recommended that further research is needed into the distinctive chemistry of *S. torminalis*.

A study by Li and team (2016) looked at the bioactivity and health benefits of wild fruits in general and concluded that such food sources are wildly underutilised. Li and team suggest that wild fruit have untapped potential to be developed into 'functional foods' or for pharmaceuticals to help prevent and treat chronic disease. The authors write: "In recent years, wild fruits have attracted increasing attention, and accumulative investigations have been performed for their bioactive effects, such as antioxidant, antimicrobial anti-inflammatory, and anticancer effects." In their study, Li and team found that Sorbus fruits showed moderate activity to inhibit AChE – a property that could help to prevent neurodegenerative diseases such as Alzheimer's.

An earlier study by Nejad and team (2013), specifically on wild fruits growing in the Heyrat region of Northern Iran, looked at current ethnobotanical uses in Iranian folk medicine, such as for laxatives, diarrhoea, inflammation, blood purification and toothache, and concluded that these wild fruits, including Sorbus fruits, have potential for many more medicinal uses. In Iranian folk medicine, wild service fruit has been used to treat coughs, bronchitis, colic, fever, diarrhoea, kidney stones, and as a diuretic.

Other studies have also noted the useful medicinal properties not only of the fruit but of the flowers, leaves and bark of Sorbus species generally, which may be used for diarrhoea, inflammatory conditions, diabetes, heart or circulatory problems and as a diuretic. Irving cites a 2008 study on the fruit of the true service specifically (*S. domestica*) which suggested that the beneficial phytochemicals of the berries might improve the health of diabetes sufferers.

SAFETY NOTE

There is little information on the possible toxicity and side effects of eating Wild Service Tree berries, or the seeds, flowers and other plant material, or of using the tree in medicine. This is not proof of its safety. Use with caution or seek medical advice if you have a medical condition or are pregnant or breastfeeding.

WOOD AVENS
Geum urbanum

FAMILY

Rosaceae.

BOTANICAL DESCRIPTION

Flowers 13mm to 19mm across, few, yellow, on long stalks, in irregular, terminal clusters. Sepals 5; bracts 5; petals 5; stamens numerous; carpels numerous. Fruits in a dense head of small, dry, 1-seeded achenes, each ending in the persistent style, which is red and hairy and is hooked at the tip. Stems 20cms to 90cms high, erect, hairy; the leaves of the root divided to the midrib into 2-4 pairs of large, coarsely-toothed leaflets, intermixed with smaller ones and one large terminal one; the leaves of the upper stem only divided into 3 leaflets (pinnately-trifoliate), with large leafy stipules.

FLOWERS

May to November.

STATUS

Perennial. Native.

HABITAT

Deciduous woodland, coniferous woodland, hedgerows, wasteland.

OVERVIEW

Wood Avens, or Herb Bennet is a woodland member of the rose family (Rosaceae).

Curiously, the plant's Latin name urbanum means 'city dweller' which is where this wild flower of hedges and woods was also once found.

The generic name Geum derives from the Greek geno meaning an agreeable fragrance.

FOOD

In 16th-century Britain, Wood Avens was a common potherb added to broths and soups, and the young leaves were sometimes used in salads. The herb's bright green colour was used by chefs in Medieval Europe for green colouring.

In the Balkans, Wood Avens is picked to add to salads or to make a condiment. In the Czech Republic, the wild herb is dried and used as a seasoning.

The roots and rhizomes are aromatic with the scent of cloves, which has led to one of the plant's common names being 'clove root'.

The rhizomes bring a hint of clove and cinnamon to soups, broths, sauces, fruit pies and stewed fruit. 'Clove root' can be combined with orange peel and added to wine, which is said to produce a pleasant Vermouth, or other mulled drinks, gin and beer.

The German Augsburg ale, for example, has a bag of clove root added to the casks to flavour the drink. Traditionally, the herb was not only used to flavour ales but also prevent the ale from souring. The roots of Wood Avens can also be boiled in milk to make a tasty Indian-style 'chai' tea. The leaves can be infused to make a hot, mildly spicy cordial.

While 'clove root' can be used as a substitute for cloves, more of the herb would be required in cooking to achieve the same aromatic effects. The leaves also have a mild clove like flavour and can be added to spicy herb salads.

Wild Greens With Spiced Tahini Rice

- 2 handfuls of boiled young Wood Avens tips
- 1 handful of boiled young ground elder leaves and stems
- 2 handfuls of raw three cornered leek (flowers, leaves and stems)
- 2 green chillies (chopped)
- 1 handful of fresh sage (chopped)
- 1 knob of butter
- 1 dash of bran oil
- 1 tsp of coconut butter
- 2 tsp cider vinegar
- 2 tbsp tahini
- 8 ozs cooked short grain brown rice

Cook the rice and set aside. Boil Wood Avens tips for five minutes, strain and chop finely. Boil ground elder leaves and stems for three minutes, strain and chop finely. Melt butter in a pan and add a dash of bran oil to prevent the butter from burning. Add the chopped chillies and fry for one minute. Add the cooked Wood Avens and ground elder and fry for three minutes, then add the three cornered leek and fresh sage, mix well. Remove from heat, add rice, coconut butter, vinegar and tahini and mix well, then serve.

Crispy Wood Avens

- 6 handfuls of Wood Avens leaves (chopped)
- 2 garlic cloves (crushed)
- Knob of butter
- Sugar (optional)

Melt butter in frying pan and fry the crushed garlic for 30 seconds. Chop the Wood Avens leaves up and add to frying pan, and gently fry until crispy. You might need to add more butter as the leaves can absorb quite a lot. Serve with spicy food.

MEDICINE

German Benedictine abbess Hildegard von Bingen (1098-1179) cautioned her readers that drinking a decoction of herb Bennet (Wood Avens) would make a person burn with lusty desire, unless that person was weak of body in which case it would help to recover their strength.

> "But after the body has gotten better, the person should avoid bennet."

Whether Hildegard's cautionary words were heeded or not, Wood Avens was used as a preservative to protect against the plague (in the form of a cordial) and as an antidote to poison; the former use was not successful (but what remedies were successful against the bubonic plague?) and the latter use may derive from the herb's connection to St Benedict.

The plant was sometimes considered a 'cure-all', again, perhaps thanks to its powerful reputation in folklore. The name 'avens' comes from the Spanish word meaning 'antidote'.

English writer John Pechey (1655-1715) wrote of Wood Avens:

> "Wine wherein the Root has been infus'd has a fine Taste and Smell: It cheers the Heart, and opens obstructions".

The roots and rhizomes have been used in traditional herbal medicine for treating various problems: gastrointestinal disorders, such as diarrhoea, dyspepsia, constipation, indigestion, stomach upsets, and appetite loss; oral disease, such as throat and mouth infections; skin complaints, such as chilblains and haemorrhoids.

The wild herb's primary use, however, appears to have been for gut complaints and to aid digestion, which is how it was prescribed by Paracelsus (1493-1541). The roots steeped in wine would "helpeth digestion - warmeth a cold stomach and open obstructions of the liver and spleen". For diarrhoea, the stringy roots were pounded to a powder added to wine which "binds the body and belly and stops all the torments thereof".

The plant was also used as a remedy for bites, fevers and internal wounds. It was also said to be a good heart stimulant. John Moncrief wrote in his Poor Man's Physician (1731) about Wood Avens: "For Inward Wounds; Drink the Decoction of Avens-roots. It prevails also for Pains in the Breast and Sides, and to dispel internal crudities." Herbalist John Gerard (1545-1612) praised the herb's virtue for removing freckles, spots, pimples and sunburn from the face.

In Ireland, Wood Avens was also a herbal remedy for kidney problems and for treating chills. In Country Cavan, a folk record identifies a herb as 'evans', which may refer to 'avens', that was used for kidney troubles.

Yet, despite its reputation as a 'cure-all', Wood Avens was not used much in British and Irish folk medicine as suggested by the lack of folk records. The records are scant. For example, in Wiltshire the herb was sometimes picked in spring to make a 'pick-me-up-tonic'; this is supposedly good for purifying the liver. But there are few other mentions to Wood Avens in local folk medicine.

Even a recommendation from English herbalist and physician Nicholas Culpeper (1616-1654) failed to make the herb a household name. He wrote:

> "It is good for the diseases of the chest or breath, for pains and stitches in the sides, it dissolveth inward congealed blood occasioned by falls and bruises and the spitting of blood, if the roots either green or dried be boiled in wine and drunk. The root in the spring-time steeped in wine doth give it a delicate flavour and taste and being drunk fasting every morning comforteth the heart and is a good preservative against the plague or any other poison. It is very safe and is fit to be kept in every body's house."

Sir John Hill in 1812 also wrote in praise of the wild herb: "I have known it [Wood Avens] alone cure intermittent fevers."

Many records of its use are gypsy in origin, such as a remedy that stews the herb in vinegar to treat sore eyes. An anecdote from Roy Vickery tells us: "The crushed root is used [by gypsies] as a cure for diarrhoea, and a little in boiling water relieves sore throats [1944]".

The Maoris called the plant kopata and chewed the leaves as a remedy for dysentery.

In modern herbal medicine, Wood Avens is largely used for mouth, gum, throat and gut irritations. Herbalists may still prescribe the dried herb or root as a tonic for general debility, chills, headaches, dyspepsia or to relax the throat. It has also been used for diarrhoea, peptic ulcers, irritable bowel syndrome, fever, nausea, vomiting, haemorrhages, and colitis.

Duke recommends Wood Avens for a number of other wide-ranging conditions, including anaemia, anorexia, asthma, as well as various types of cancer and infectious disease such as cholera.

Bartrams also indicates its use for Crohn's disease. It is recommended that you seek the advice of your doctor before using a medicinal plant such as Wood Avens to treat any of these conditions.

The aromatic roots actually contain eugenol - the main chemical constituent of clove oil, the essential oil distilled from cloves (*Syzygium aromaticum*). Polish researchers (2011) found that the eugenol content in 'clove root' is not affected by the age of the plant or time of harvest; although in times past it was believed that the best time to pick the roots was on 25 March (see the Folklore section). The roots also contain tannins and another bitter substance.

The actions of the roots are tonic, astringent, stomachic and febrifuge (in the case of the latter, the herb is said to have a quinine-like action for lowering fever and has been used as a substitute for Peruvian bark); externally they are vulnerary (wound healer). The leaves too are slightly astringent.

The plant is also slightly anaesthetic and antiseptic, as well as anti-inflammatory. It has also been used as a douche for excessive vaginal discharge. As a cosmetic, an infusion of Wood Avens may be used to treat spots and freckles.

In parts of Europe, the Wood Avens is still harvested as a medicinal herb, such as in the Balkans where it is used for oral and digestive complaints, loss of appetite and haemorrhoids.

It is unsurprising that Wood Avens is an astringent herb being a member of the rose (Rosaceae) family which is known for its astringency. Herbalist David Hoffman explains that the astringent constituents contain tannins that temporarily coat bodily tissue and create a barrier to infection that reduces irritation and inflammation. This makes astringent herbs useful as wound healers and for soothing gut irritations that may cause diarrhoea and dysentery.

A study by Paun and team (2015) concluded that *G. urbanum* has neuroprotective effects. The plant contains enzymes that inhibits neurodegenerative disease and displays antioxidant activity against the inflammatory effects of such illnesses.

A more recent study by Dimtrova and team (2017) concluded that G. urbanum has antimicrobial activity against certain Gram-positive bacteria, in addition to significant antioxidant activity against free-radicals, making it a potential medicinal plant.

SAFETY NOTE

Because of its high tannin content, some texts recommend that the herb is not used in large quantities. It may also be safer to avoid during pregnancy or when breastfeeding.

ABOUT THE AUTHOR

Robin Harford established his wild food foraging school in 2008, and his foraging courses are listed at the top of BBC Countryfile's 'Best foraging courses in the UK'.

He is the creator of eatweeds.co.uk. Michelin chef Richard Corrigen recommended the site for inclusion in The Times Top 50 Websites For Food and Drink.

Robin has travelled extensively, documenting and recording wild food plants' traditional and local uses in indigenous cultures. His work has taken him to Africa, India, SE Asia, Europe and the USA.

Occasionally he appears on national and local radio and television.

His work has been recommended in BBC Good Food magazine, Sainsbury's magazine, The Guardian, The Times, The Independent, The Daily Telegraph, etc.

He is a member of the Society for Ethnobotany and the Botanical Society of Britain and Ireland.

instagram.com/eatweedsuk
facebook.com/eatweedsuk

BIBLIOGRAPHY

Allen, D. E. & Hatfield, G. (2004) *Medicinal Plants in Folk Tradition: An Ethnobotany of Britain & Ireland*. Portland: Timber Press.

Altschul, S. von R. (2013) *Drugs and Foods from Little-Known Plants: Notes in Harvard University Herbaria*. Harvard University Press.

Ambasta, S. (2000) *The Useful Plants of India*. New Delhi: National Institute of Science Communication, Council of Scientific & Industrial Research.

Badhwar, R. L. & Fernandez, R. R. (2011) *Edible Wild Plants of the Himalayas*. Delhi: Daya Pub. House.

Baïracli-Levy, J. de & Wood, H. (1997) *Common Herbs for Natural Health*. Woodstock, N.Y.: Ash Tree Publishing.

Baker, M. (2008) *Discovering the Folklore of Plants*. Oxford: Shire Publications.

Barnes, J. et al. (2013) *Herbal Medicines*. 4. rev. ed. London: Pharmaceutical Press.

Barros, L. et al. (2011) Exotic Fruits as a Source of Important Phytochemicals: Improving the Traditional Use of Rosa Canina Fruits in Portugal. *Food Research International.* [Online] 44 (7), 2233–2236.

Barros, L. et al. (2010) Strawberry-Tree, Blackthorn and Rose Fruits: Detailed Characterisation in Nutrients and Phytochemicals with Antioxidant Properties. *Food Chemistry.* [Online] 120 (1), 247–254.

Bartram, T. (1998) *Bartram's Encyclopedia of Herbal Medicine.* New York: Marlowe.

Basile, A. et al. (2000) Antibacterial and Allelopathic Activity of Extract from Castanea sativa Leaves. *Fitoterapia.* [Online] 71S110–S116.

Bennet, S. (1991) *Food from Forests.* Dehradun, India: Indian Council of Forestry Research and Education.

Bir, S. (2018) *The Fruit Forager's Companion: Ferments, Desserts, Main Dishes, and More from Your Neighborhood and Beyond.* Vermont: Chelsea Green Publishing.

Bryan, J. E. & Castle, C. (1974) *The Edible Ornamental Garden.* San Francisco: 101 Productions.

Burrows, I. (2011) *Food from the Wild.* London: New Holland.

Calliste, C.-A. et al. (2005) Castanea sativa Mill. Leaves as New Sources of Natural Antioxidant: An Electronic Spin Resonance Study. *Journal of Agricultural and Food Chemistry.* [Online] 53 (2), 282–288.

Carocho, M., Barros, L., et al. (2014) Castanea sativa Mill. Flowers Amongst the Most Powerful Antioxidant Matrices: A Phytochemical Approach in Decoctions and Infusions. *BioMed Research International.* [Online] 20141-7.

Carocho, M., Calhelha, R. C., et al. (2014) Infusions and Decoctions of Castanea sativa Flowers as Effective Antitumor and Antimicrobial Matrices. *Industrial Crops and Products.* [Online] 6242-46.

Chiarini, A. et al. (2013) Sweet Chestnut (Castanea sativa Mill.) Bark Extract: Cardiovascular Activity and Myocyte Protection Against Oxidative Damage. *Oxidative Medicine and Cellular Longevity.* [Online] 20131-10.

Christaki, E. (2012) Hippophae rhamnoides L. (Sea Buckthorn): A Potential Source of Nutraceuticals. *Food and Public Health.* [Online] 269-72.

Cleene, M. de & Lejeune, M. C. (2002) *Compendium of Symbolic and Ritual Plants in Europe.* Ghent: Man & Culture.

Conway, P. (2002) *Tree Medicine: A Comprehensive Guide to the Healing Power of Over 170 Trees.* London: Piatkus.

Couplan, F. (2009) *Le Régal Végétal: Plantes Sauvages Comestibles.* Paris: Sang de la Terre.

Couplan, F. (1998) *The Encyclopedia of Edible Plants of North America.* New Canaan: Keats Pub.

Courter, J. W. & Rhodes, A. M. (1969) Historical Notes on Horseradish. *Economic Botany.* 23 (2), 156-164.

Cruz, B. R. et al. (2013) Chemical Composition and Functional Properties of Native Chestnut Starch (Castanea sativa Mill). *Carbohydrate Polymers.* [Online] 94 (1), 594-602.

Culpeper, N. (1841) *Culpeper's Complete Herbal.* London: J.S. Pratt.

Curtis, T. et al. (2019) *The Wild Food Plants of Ireland: The Complete Guide to Their Recognition, Foraging, Cooking, History and Conservation*. Ireland: Orla Kelly Publishing.

De Natale, A. & Pollio, A. (2012) A Forgotten Collection: The Libyan Ethnobotanical Exhibits (1912-14) by a. Trotter at the Museum O. Comes at the University Federico Ii in Naples, Italy. *Journal of Ethnobiology and Ethnomedicine.* [Online] 8 (1), 4.

De Vasconcelos, M. C. et al. (2010) Composition of European Chestnut (Castanea sativa Mill.) and Association with Health Effects: Fresh and Processed Products. *Journal of the Science of Food and Agriculture.* [Online] 90 (10), 1578–1589.

Dhyani, D. et al. (2007) Basic Nutritional Attributes of Hippophae rhamnoides (seabuckthorn) Populations from Uttarakhand Himalaya, India. *Current science.* 92 1148–1152.

Dimitrova, L. et al. (2017) Antimicrobial and Antioxidant Potential of Different Solvent Extracts of the Medicinal Plant Geum urbanum L. *Chemistry Central Journal.* [Online] 11 (1), 113.

Doukani, K. & Hadjer, M. (2015) Physico-Chemical and Nutritional Characterization of Arbutus Unedo L. from the Region of Tiaret (algeria). *International Journal of Humanities, Arts, Medicine and Sciences.* 3 1–14.

Duke, J. A. (1992) *CRC Handbook of Edible Weeds*. Boca Raton: CRC Press.

Duke, J. A. (1985) *CRC Handbook of Medicinal Herbs*. Boca Raton: CRC Press.

Egea, I. et al. (2010) Six Edible Wild Fruits as Potential Antioxidant Additives or Nutritional Supplements. *Plant Foods for Human Nutrition.* [Online] 65 (2), 121–129.

Ehrlich, G. & Hozeski, B. W. (2001) *Hildegard's Healing Plants: From Her Medieval Classic Physica*. Boston: Beacon Press.

Eland, S. C. & Lucas, G. (2013) *Plant Biographies*.

Elias, T. S. & Dykeman, P. A. (2009) *Edible Wild Plants: A North American Field Guide to Over 200 Natural Foods*. New York: Sterling.

Ercisli, S. (2007) Chemical Composition of Fruits in Some Rose (Rosa Spp.) Species. *Food Chemistry*. [Online] 104 (4), 1379–1384.

Facciola, S. (1998) *Cornucopia II: A Source Book of Edible Plants*. Vista, CA: Kampong Publications.

Fernald, M. L. et al. (1996) *Edible Wild Plants of Eastern North America*. New York: Dover Publications.

Ferreira, I. C. F. R. et al. (eds.) (2017) *Wild Plants, Mushrooms and Nuts: Functional Food Properties and Applications*. Chichester: Wiley Blackwell.

Fleischhauer, S. G. et al. (2014) *Enzyklopädie Essbare Wildpflanzen: 2000 Pflanzen Mitteleuropas; Bestimmung, Sammeltipps, Inhaltsstoffe, Heilwirkung, Verwendung in Der Küche*. Aarau München: AT-Verl.

Folkard, R. (1884) *Plant Lore, Legends, and Lyrics*. London: Sampson Low, Marston, Searle, and Rivington.

Fonseca, D. et al. (2015) Bioactive Phytochemicals from Wild Arbutus unedo L. Berries from Different Locations in Portugal: Quantification of Lipophilic Components. *International Journal of Molecular Sciences*. [Online] 16 (12), 14194–14209.

Frohne, D. & Pfänder, H. J. (1984) *A Colour Atlas of Poisonous Plants: A Handbook for Pharmacists, Doctors, Toxicologists, and Biologists*. A Wolfe science book. London: Wolfe Pub.

Gardner, Z. E. et al. (eds.) (2013) *American Herbal Products Association's Botanical Safety Handbook*. Boca Raton: CRC Press.

Gerard, J. (1994) *Gerard's Herbal: The History of Plants*. Nachdruck. Marcus Woodward (ed.). London: Senate, an imprint of Studio Editions Ltd.

Gibbons, E. (1987) *Stalking the Wild Asparagus*. Woodstock: A.C. Hood.

Gironés-Vilaplana, A. et al. (2013) New Isotonic Drinks with Antioxidant and Biological Capacities from Berries (maqui, Açaí and Blackthorn) and Lemon Juice. *International Journal of Food Sciences and Nutrition*. [Online] 64 (7), 897–906.

Gonciarz, W. (n.d.) *Analysis of Anti-CCRL1 Antibodies in Human Sera Using Quantitative Dot Blot Method* [online]. Available from: https://www.researchgate.net/publication/284899021_ANALY SIS_OF_ANTI-CCRL1_ANTIBODIES_IN_HUMAN_SERA_US ING_QUANTITATIVE_DOT_BLOT_METHOD (Accessed 10 October 2019).

Gray, P. (2002) *Honey from a Weed: Fasting and Feasting in Tuscany, Catalonia, the Cyclades, and Apulia*. Paperback ed. Devon, England: Prospect Books.

Grieve, M. M. (1998) *A Modern Herbal*. London: Tiger Books International.

Grigson, G. (1996) *The Englishman's Flora*. Oxford: Helicon.

Haines, A. (2010) *Ancestral Plants Volume 1: A Primitive Skills Guide to Important Edible, Medicinal, and Useful Plants*. Southwest Harbor: Anaskimin.

Haines, A. (2015) *Ancestral Plants Volume 2: A Primitive Skills Guide to Important Edible, Medicinal, and Useful Plants of the Northwest*. Vol. 2. Korea: Anaskimin.

Hasbal, G. et al. (2015) Antioxidant and Antiacetylcholinesterase Activities of Sorbus torminalis (l.) Crantz (Wild Service Tree) Fruits. *Journal of Food and Drug Analysis*. [Online] 23 (1), 57–62.

Hatfield, G. (2004) *Encyclopedia of Folk Medicine: Old World and New World Traditions*. Santa Barbara, Calif: ABC-CLIO.

Hatfield, G. (2008) *Hatfield's Herbal: The Secret History of British Plants*. London: Penguin.

Henslow, G. (1905) *The Uses of British Plants Traced from Antiquity to the Present Day*. Ashford, Kent: L. Reeve & Co., Ltd.

Hu, S. (2005) *Food Plants of China*. Hong Kong: Chinese University Press.

Irving, M. (2009) *The Forager Handbook: A Guide to the Edible Plants of Britain*. London: Ebury.

Jarić, S. et al. (2007) An Ethnobotanical Study on the Usage of Wild Medicinal Herbs from Kopaonik Mountain (central Serbia). *Journal of Ethnopharmacology*. [Online] 111 (1), 160–175.

Jman Redzic, S. (2006) Wild Edible Plants and Their Traditional Use in the Human Nutrition in Bosnia-Herzegovina. *Ecology of Food and Nutrition*. [Online] 45 (3), 189–232.

Kalle, R. & Soukand, R. (2012) Historical Ethnobotanical Review of Wild Edible Plants of Estonia (1770s-1960s). *Acta Societatis Botanicorum Poloniae*. 81 (4), . [online]. Available from: http://yadda.icm.edu.pl/yadda/element/bwmeta1.element.agro-2f98db46-5557-44e4-b8c1-2704c26b85b9 (Accessed 19 March 2019).

Karalliedde, L. et al. (2008) *Traditional Herbal Medicines: A Guide to Their Safer Use*. London: Hammersmith.

Kermath, BM et al. (2013) *Food Plants in the Americas: A Survey of the Domesticated, Cultivated, and Wild Plants Used for Human Food in North, Central and South America and the Caribbean*.

Kershaw, L. (2017) *Edible & Medicinal Plants of the Rockies*.

Kiple, K. F. & Ornelas, K. C. (eds.) (2000) *The Cambridge World History of Food*. Cambridge: Cambridge University Press.

Kirkeskov, B. et al. (2011) The Effects of Rose Hip (rosa Canina) on Plasma Antioxidative Activity and C-Reactive Protein in Patients with Rheumatoid Arthritis and Normal Controls: A Prospective Cohort Study. *Phytomedicine*. [Online] 18 (11), 953–958.

Kizilarslan, Ç. (2012) An Ethnobotanical Study of the Useful and Edible Plants of Izmit. *Marmara Pharmaceutical Journal*. [Online] 3 (16), 194–200.

Kosňovsk, J. (2013) The Origin, Archaeobotany and Ethnobotany of Sweet Chestnut (Castanea sativa Miller) in the Czech Republic. *Interdisciplinaria Archaeologica - Natural Sciences in Archaeology*. 163–176.

Kress, H. (2011) *Practical Herbs*. 1st edition. Yrtit ja yrttiterapia Henriette Kress.

Kristbergsson, K. & Jorge, O. (2015) *Traditional Foods*. New York: Springer.

Kuhnlein, H. V. & Turner, N. J. (1991) *Traditional Plant Foods of Canadian Indigenous Peoples: Nutrition, Botany, and Use*. Food and nutrition in history and anthropology v. 8. Philadelphia: Gordon and Breach.

Kültür, Ş. (2008) An Ethnobotanical Study of Kırklareli (Turkey). *PHYTOLOGIA BALCANICA*. 14279–289.

Kunkel, G. (1984) *Plants for Human Consumption: An Annotated Checklist of the Edible Phanerogams and Ferns*. Koenigstein: Koeltz Scientific Books.

Lang, D. C. (1987) *The Complete Book of British Berries*. London: Threshold Books.

Le Strange, R. (1977) *A History of Herbal Plants*. London: Angus and Robertson.

Lentini, F. & Venza, F. (2007) Wild Food Plants of Popular Use in Sicily. *Journal of Ethnobiology and Ethnomedicine*. [Online] 315.

Li, Y. et al. (2016) Bioactivities and Health Benefits of Wild Fruits. *International Journal of Molecular Sciences*. [Online] 17 (8), 1258.

Lim, T. K. (2016) *Edible Medicinal and Non Medicinal Plants. Volume 9, Modified Stems, Roots, Bulbs*.

Lim, T. K. (2012) *Edible Medicinal and Non-Medicinal Plants. Vol. 4: Fruits*. Dordrecht: Springer.

Lim, T.K. (2012) *Edible Medicinal and Non-Medicinal Plants: Volume 1, Fruits*. Dordrecht: Springer.

Łuczaj, Ł. et al. (2013) Wild Food Plants Used in the Villages of the Lake Vrana Nature Park (northern Dalmatia, Croatia). *Acta Societatis Botanicorum Poloniae*. [Online] 82275–281.

Luczaj, L. & Szymanski, W. M. (2007) Wild Vascular Plants Gathered for Consumption in the Polish Countryside: A Review. *Journal of Ethnobiology and Ethnomedicine*. [Online] 3 (1), 17.

Mabey, R. (1977) *Plants with a Purpose: A Guide to the Everyday Uses of Wild Plants*. London: Collins.

Mabey, R. & Blamey, M. (1974) *Food for Free*. London: Collins.

Mac Coitir, N. & Langrishe, G. (2015) *Ireland's Wild Plants: Myths, Legends and Folklore*.

Manandhar, N. P. & Manandhar, S. (2002) *Plants and People of Nepal*. Portland: Timber Press.

Marzocco, S. et al. (2015) Anti-Inflammatory Activity of Horseradish (Armoracia rusticana) Root Extracts in Lps-Stimulated Macrophages. *Food & Function*. [Online] 6 (12), 3778–3788.

Menendez-Baceta, G. et al. (2012) Wild Edible Plants Traditionally Gathered in Gorbeialdea (biscay, Basque Country). *Genetic Resources and Crop Evolution*. [Online] 59 (7), 1329–1347.

Michael, P. (1980) *All Good Things Around Us: A Cookbook and Guide to Wild Plants and Herbs*. 1st American ed. New York: Holt, Rinehart, and Winston.

Michael, P. & King, C. (2015) *Edible Wild Plants & Herbs: A Compendium of Recipes and Remedies*. Paperback edition. London: Grub Street.

Mikulic-Petkovsek, M. et al. (2017) Bioactive Components and Antioxidant Capacity of Fruits from Nine Sorbus Genotypes. *Journal of Food Science*. [Online] 82 (3), 647–658.

Mills, S. Y. & Bone, K. (eds.) (2005) *The Essential Guide to Herbal Safety*. St. Louis: Elsevier Churchill Livingstone.

Moffet, L. (1992) Fruits, Vegetables, Herbs and Other Plants from the Latrine at Dudley Castle in Central England, Used by the Royalist Garrison During the Civil War. *Review of Palaeobotany and Palynology*. [Online] 73 (1), 271–286.

Molina, M. et al. (2011) Fruit Production of Strawberry Tree (Arbutus unedo L.) in Two Spanish Forests. *Forestry*. [Online] 84 (4), 419–429.

Mozaffari Nejad, A. S. et al. (2013) Ethnobotany and Folk Medicinal Uses of Major Trees and Shrubs in Northern Iran. *Journal of medicinal plant research*. [Online] 7284–289.

Mustafa, B. et al. (2012) Medical Ethnobotany of the Albanian Alps in Kosovo. *Journal of Ethnobiology and Ethnomedicine*. [Online] 8 (1), 6.

Nedelcheva, A. (2013) An Ethnobotanical Study of Wild Edible Plants in Bulgaria. *EurAsian Journal of BioSciences*. [Online] 777–94.

Neves, J. (2018) Castanea sativa Mill. Extract Cytotoxicity. *European Journal of Medicinal Plants*. [Online] 24 (3), 1–4.

Newall, C. A. et al. (1996) *Herbal Medicines: A Guide for Health-Care Professionals*. London: Pharmaceutical Press.

Nyerges, C. & Begley, E. (2014) *Guide to Wild Foods and Useful Plants*. Chicago Review Press.

Olszewska, M. A. (2011) In Vitro Antioxidant Activity and Total Phenolic Content of the Inflorescences, Leaves and Fruits of Sorbus torminalis (l.) Crantz. *Acta Poloniae Pharmaceutica*. 68 (6), 945–953.

Özcan, M. (2002) Nutrient Composition of Rose (rosa Canina L.) Seed and Oils. *Journal of Medicinal Food*. [Online] 5 (3), 137–140.

Ozcan, T. et al. (2017) Antioxidant Properties of Probiotic Fermented Milk Supplemented with Chestnut Flour (Castanea sativa Mill). *Journal of Food Processing and Preservation*. [Online] 41 (5), e13156.

Ozturk, M. et al. (2018) A Comparative Analysis of Medicinal and Aromatic Plants Used in the Traditional Medicine of Iğdir (Turkey), Nakhchivan (Azerbaijan), and Tabriz (Iran). *Pakistan Journal of Botany*. 50(1).

Paine, A. (2006) *The Healing Power of Celtic Plants: Their History, Their Use, and the Scientific Evidence That They Work*. Winchester: O Books.

Park, H.-W. et al. (2013) Antimicrobial Activity of Isothiocyanates (ITCs) Extracted from Horseradish (Armoracia rusticana) Root Against Oral Microorganisms. *Biocontrol Science*. [Online] 18 (3), 163–168.

Paun, G. et al. (2015) Inhibitory Potential of Some Romanian Medicinal Plants Against Enzymes Linked to Neurodegenerative Diseases and Their Antioxidant Activity. *Pharmacognosy Magazine*. [Online] 11 (42), 110.

Pawera, L. et al. (2017) Traditional Plant Knowledge in the White Carpathians: Ethnobotany of Wild Food Plants and Crop Wild Relatives in the Czech Republic. *Human Ecology*. [Online] 45 (5), 655–671.

Pedersen, M. (2010) *Nutritional Herbology: A Reference Guide to Herbs*. Warsaw: Whitman Publications.

Pennacchio, M. et al. (2010) *Uses and Abuses of Plant-Derived Smoke: It's Ethnobotany as Hallucinogen, Perfume, Incense, and Medicine*. New York: Oxford University Press.

Phondani, P. C. et al. (2010) *Ethnobotanical Uses of Plants among the Bhotiya Tribal Communities of Niti Valley in Central Himalaya, India*. [online]. Available from: http://scholarspace.manoa.hawaii.edu/handle/10125/21011 (Accessed 2 October 2019).

Pieroni, A. (2003) Ethnobotanical Knowledge of the Istro-Romanians of Zejane in Croatia. *Fitoterapia*. [Online] 74 (7–8), 710–719.

Pieroni, A. (ed.) (2014) *Ethnobotany and Biocultural Diversities in the Balkans: Perspectives on Sustainable Rural Development and Reconciliation*. New York: Springer.

Prior, R. (1863) *On the Popular Names of British Plants: Being an Explanation of the Origin and Meaning of the Names of Our Indigenous and Most Commonly Cultivated Species*. London: Williams and Norgate.

Pujol, C. A. et al. (2016) The Antiviral Potency of Fagus Sylvatica 4ome-Glucuronoxylan Sulfates. *International journal of biological macromolecules*. [Online] 87 195–200.

Quattrocchi, U. (2012) *CRC World Dictionary of Medicinal and Poisonous Plants: Common Names, Scientific Names, Eponyms, Synonyms, and Etymology (5 Volume Set)*. Boca Raton: CRC press.

Quave, C. L. & Pieroni, A. (2015) A Reservoir of Ethnobotanical Knowledge Informs Resilient Food Security and Health Strategies in the Balkans. *Nature Plants*. [Online] 1 (2), 14021.

Redzić, S. (2010) Use of Wild and Semi-Wild Edible Plants in Nutrition and Survival of People in 1430 Days of Siege of Sarajevo During the War in Bosnia and Herzegovina (1992-1995). *Collegium Antropologicum*. 34 (2), 551–570.

Richards, J. F. (2005) *The Unending Frontier: An Environmental History of the Early Modern World*. The California world history library 1. Berkeley: University of California Press.

Richardson, A. T. et al. (2020) Discovery of a Stable Vitamin C Glycoside in Crab Apples (Malus sylvestris). *Phytochemistry*. [Online] 173 112297.

Rop, O. et al. (2010) Antioxidant Properties of European Cranberrybush Fruit (Viburnum opulus var. edule). *Molecules*. [Online] 15 (6), 4467–4477.

Ruiz-Rodríguez, B.-M. et al. (2011) Valorization of Wild Strawberry-Tree Fruits (Arbutus unedo L.) Through Nutritional Assessment and Natural Production Data. *Food Research International*. [Online] 44 (5), 1244–1253.

Runyon, L. (2007) *The Essential Wild Food Survival Guide*. Shiloh: Wild Food Company.

Sagdic, O. et al. (2006) Evaluation of the Antibacterial and Antioxidant Potentials of Cranberry (Gilaburu, Viburnum opulus L.) Fruit Extract. *Acta Alimentaria*. [Online] 35 (4), 487–492.

Sampliner, D. & Miller, A. (2009) Ethnobotany of Horseradish (Armoracia rusticana , Brassicaceae) and Its Wild Relatives (Armoracia spp.): Reproductive Biology and Local Uses in Their Native Ranges. *Economic Botany*. 63 (3), 303–313.

Sánchez-Mata, M. de C. & Tardío, J. (eds.) (2016) *Mediterranean Wild Edible Plants: Ethnobotany and Food Composition Tables*. [Online]. New York: Springer.

Sarli Giulio et al. (2016) Collecting Landraces of Vegetable Crop Species in the South-West Romania. *Journal of Environmental Science and Engineering B*. [Online] 5 (1), .

Serteser, A. et al. (2009) Antioxidant Properties of Some Plants Growing Wild in Turkey. *Grasas y Aceites*. [Online] 60 (2), 147–154.

Sharma, H. & Meredith, A. D. (2004) A Report of 18 Blackthorn Injuries of the Upper Limb. *Injury*. [Online] 35 (9), 930–935.

Shikov, A. N. et al. (2017) Traditional and Current Food Use of Wild Plants Listed in the Russian Pharmacopoeia. *Frontiers in Pharmacology*. [Online] 8841.

Simkova, K. & Polesny, Z. (2015) Ethnobotanical Review of Wild Edible Plants Used in the Czech Republic. *Journal of Applied Botany and Food Quality*. 88 (1), .

Small, E. (2006) *Culinary Herbs*. 2nd ed. Ottawa: NRC Research Press.

Smith, J. R. (2013) *Tree Crops: A Permanent Agriculture*. Island Press.

Sõukand, R. & Kalle, R. (2016) *Changes in the Use of Wild Food Plants in Estonia: 18th-21st Century*. SpringerBriefs in Plant Science. 1st ed. 2016. [Online]. Cham: Springer.

Sturtevant, E. L. (1972) *Sturtevant's Edible Plants of the World*. New York: Dover Publications.

Sulusoglu, M. et al. (2011) Arbutus unedo L. (Strawberry Tree) Selection in Turkey Samanli Mountain Locations. *Journal of Medicinal Plants Research*. 5.

Suryakumar, G. & Gupta, A. (2011) Medicinal and Therapeutic Potential of Sea Buckthorn (hippophae rhamnoides L.). *Journal of Ethnopharmacology*. [Online] 138 (2), 268–278.

Svanberg, I. (2012) The Use of Wild Plants as Food in Pre-Industrial Sweden. *Acta Societatis Botanicorum Poloniae*. [Online] 81317–327.

Tardío, J. et al. (2005) Wild Food Plants Traditionally Used in the Province of Madrid, Central Spain. *Economic Botany*. [Online] 59 (2), 122.

Tavares, L. et al. (2010) Antioxidant and Antiproliferative Properties of Strawberry Tree Tissues. *Journal of Berry Research.* [Online] (1), 3–12.

Thayer, S. (2010) *Nature's Garden: A Guide to Identifying, Harvesting, and Preparing Edible Wild Plants.* Birchwood: Forager's Harvest.

Tilford, G. L. (1997) *Edible and Medicinal Plants of the West.* Missoula: Mountain Press Pub.

Tiong, W. H. C. & Butt, F. S. (2009) Subcutaneous Emphysema of the Upper Extremity Following Penetrating Blackthorn Injury to the Wrist. *Journal of plastic, reconstructive & aesthetic surgery: JPRAS.* 62 (2), e29-32.

Turner, N. J. (1981) A Gift for the Taking: The Untapped Potential of Some Food Plants of North American Native Peoples. *Canadian Journal of Botany.* [Online] 59 (11), 2331–2357.

Turner, N. J. et al. (2011) Edible and Tended Wild Plants, Traditional Ecological Knowledge and Agroecology. *Critical Reviews in Plant Sciences.* [Online] 30 (1–2), 198–225.

Uphof, J. C. T. (1959) *Dictionary of Economic Plants.* New York: H.R. Engelmann.

Usher, G. (1974) *A Dictionary of Plants Used by Man.* London: Constable.

Vaughan, J. G. et al. (2009) *The New Oxford Book of Food Plants.* Oxford: Oxford University Press.

Vickery, R. (1997) *A Dictionary of Plant-Lore.* Oxford: Oxford University Press.

Vickery, R. (2019) *Vickery's Folk Flora: An a-Z of the Folklore and Uses of British and Irish Plants.* London: Weidenfeld & Nicolson.

Wani, T. A. et al. (2016) Bioactive Profile, Health Benefits and Safety Evaluation of Sea Buckthorn (Hippophae rhamnoides L.): A Review Fatih Yildiz (ed.). *Cogent Food & Agriculture*. 2 (1).

Warren, P. (2006) *British Native Trees: Their Past and Present Uses: Including a Guide to Burning Wood in the Home*. Dereham? Wildeye.

Watts, D. (2007) *Dictionary of Plant Lore*. Amsterdam: Elsevier.

Welk, E. et al. (2016) '*Sorbus torminalis* in Europe: Distribution, Habitat, Usage and Threats', in p.

Wetzel, S. et al. (2006) *Bioproducts from Canada's Forests: New Partnerships in the Bioeconomy*. Dordrecht: Springer.

Wiersema, J. H. & Leon, B. (2013) *World Economic Plants: A Standard Reference*. Boca Raton: CRC Press.

Wyse Jackson, P. (2013) *Ireland's Generous Nature: The Past and Present Uses of Wild Plants in Ireland*. St. Louis: Missouri Botanical Garden Press.

Yance, D. R. (2013) *Adaptogens in Medical Herbalism: Elite Herbs and Natural Compounds for Mastering Stress, Aging, and Chronic Disease*. Rochester, Vermont: Healing Arts Press.

Yewlett, A. et al. (2009) Retained Blackthorn Causing Peroneal Tendonitis: A Case Report. *Foot and Ankle Surgery*. [Online] 15 (4), 205–206.

Živković, J. et al. (2010) Scavenging Capacity of Superoxide Radical and Screening of Antimicrobial Activity of Castanea sativa Mill. Extracts. *Czech Journal of Food Sciences*. [Online] 28 (No. 1), 61–68.